THE NATURAL WAY TO LEARN

THE APPRENTICESHIP APPROACH TO LITERACY

BOOK ONE
Reading

BOOK TWO
Saying Written Words Aloud

BOOK THREE
Making Things with Words and Things

Felicity Craig

Published in 1990 by
The Self Publishing Association Ltd
Lloyds Bank Chambers
Upton-upon-Severn, Worcestershire
A MEMBER OF

in conjunction with
ONE-TO-ONE Publications
33 Newcomen Road
Dartmouth, S. Devon

British Library Cataloguing in Publication Data
Craig, Felicity
    The Natural Way to Learn: the apprenticeship approach to
    literacy.
    1. Children. Reading skills. Teaching by parents
    I. Title
    428.407

ISBN 1 85421 068 8 Hardback

THE NATURAL WAY TO LEARN series is also available as three separate paperback booklets from One-to-One Publications, 33 Newcomen Road, Dartmouth, S. Devon TQ6 9BN. Prices:

Book One, **Reading**... £3.25
Book Two, **Saying Written Words Aloud**............................ £3.25
Book Three, **Making Things with Words and Things**........... £3.50

Produced and Designed by The Self Publishing Association Ltd
Printed and Bound in Great Britain by Billing & Sons Ltd, Worcester

Acknowledgements

To Keith Topping, The Paired Learning Project, Oastler Centre, 103 New Street, Huddersfield HD1 2UA, for permission to use the material on Cued Spelling given in Book Three.

I have applied for permission to quote from *Philosophy in a New Key*, by Susanne Langer (Harvard University Press), and to reproduce the diagram showing left– and right-handed positions for writing, from *Reading, Writing and Speech Problems in Children*, by Samuel Torrey Orton (W.W. Norton and Co.)

To my colleagues at Dartmouth Community college, who put up with my exasperating enthusiasm, even to the extent of becoming hooked themselves.

And to my special children, and their parents, who taught me most.

To Liz Waterland

and

all her apprentices

THE NATURAL WAY TO LEARN

THE APPRENTICESHIP APPROACH TO LITERACY

BOOK ONE

Understanding Print

READING

Felicity Craig

CONTENTS BOOK 1

Illustrated by
Lee Barlow, Darrell Parkin, John Scott

THE NATURAL WAY TO LEARN: THE APPRENTICESHIP
APPROACH TO LITERACY

Introduction to the series

This series is written for parents, for three reasons.

One is that you, as a parent, are your child's best teacher. Depending on the age of your child, you may well have already taught him to feed himself, wash himself, dress himself, swim, ride a bicycle. You have done all this without really thinking about it – by doing it for him to begin with, making it fun, and encouraging him to take over more and more, until at last he can do it by himself.

The second reason is that learning to read and write are not nearly such difficult activities as many people think. In fact written language works exactly like spoken language – so if your child can understand words he hears, he can just as easily understand words he sees. All you have to do is to help him to 'see their meanings' – by reading irresistible books to him and with him, holding the book so he can see the print, and pointing to the words as you go along. His brain is beautifully designed to understand words of any kind, whether they are spoken or written. And once he has learned to enjoy reading, he will find it very easy to learn to write.

The third reason is that a child's parents are the only adults who oversee the entire period of his growing up. You are there in his infancy and his early childhood, the pre-teen years and his adolescence. Class teachers come and go, but you witness his very first encounter with written words, and the hours he spends wrestling with his course work for G.C.S.E. So you are ideally posted to travel with him at every stage of his journey to total literacy, the place he reaches when he can read anything he wants to read, and write anything he wants to write. Also, we are coming to recognize that it is during the pre-school years when the most important foundations for fluent literacy are laid down; that simply by sharing and enjoying books with their children, parents can help infants and toddlers to learn more than any teacher ever can.

This is where my experience may be useful. I have watched my own daughters learn to read and write at the ages of three and two; and I have worked with 16+ candidates whose only barrier between them and an 'O' level grade in English Language was their spelling and punctuation. (They got their 'O' levels!) As I have travelled with many children, of all ages, I have found that the road to literacy is the same for every human being: the individual journey is unique. And no matter how old your child might be when you realize that he is struggling, or whatever the barriers in his way, you can remove all the stress and anxiety from his course, and help him to stride along enthusiastically, enjoyably and confidently.

There are only four stages on the road to complete literacy, most of them overlapping to some extent.

STAGE ONE – UNDERSTANDING PRINT

This is real reading – ways of helping both hearing and deaf children to do it are described in Book One – *Reading*.

STAGE TWO – SEEING SOUNDS, HEARING SHAPES

Or, saying written words aloud! This is a totally separate process from reading, although many people think it is the same thing. It's a sort of 'spin-off' from real reading – delightfully satisfying to do; but a child doesn't *have* to be able to say written words aloud in order to read them.

Reading aloud has far more to do with accurate spelling than with 'real reading'. So if spelling is a worry, teaching your child how to tally print with speech is the place to begin.

Ways of helping both hearing and deaf children to do this are described in Book Two – *Saying Written Words Aloud*.

STAGE THREE – GENERATING WRITTEN WORDS

Generating spoken words makes you a communicator; generating written words makes you immortal. To every fluent reader comes the moment of breathless discovery when he realizes that he too can be an author, and make written words himself. You can help your child towards this discovery, by 'writing down the ideas out of his head', until he can write them down for himself.

Many children have peculiar difficulty with writing and spelling. You will be able to nip any problems in the bud by teaching your child a particularly helpful style of handwriting, and a simple method of remembering difficult spellings. It's an interesting fact that children who have problems with spelling are also likely to be good at: drawing, painting, modelling, sculpture, technical drawing, electronics, computer programming, chess. This is no coincidence – ability in these areas does seem to 'go with the territory': so start to look out for it and encourage it. These four booklets have all been illustrated by children I work with who have spelling difficulties.

Ways of helping your child to write, and illustrate his own work, are described in Book Three – *Making Things with Words and Things*.

STAGE FOUR – PROOFREADING

Sometimes children can write their hearts out in a story, or a poem, just to find that their work is not well received because of the spelling and punctuation. They need to learn to read through their own writing so as to identify and correct any mistakes. This involves specific techniques which can be demonstrated. Again, the idea is for you to help by proofreading a *good* piece of work with your child, and showing him what to do, until he can do it by himself.

The necessary techniques are described in Book Four – Get it Write: *Learning to Proofread*. This booklet has not yet been completed, but should be available some time in 1991.

You may notice that most of the time I have talked about 'learning' rather than 'teaching'. This is because you are not going to be a 'teacher' in the formal, classroom sense. (When you are working with only one child, you don't need to be.) What you are going to do, rather, is to help your child to *learn*. Your child loves learning and wants to learn – just make the right materials available, in the right way, and you will not be able to stop him. The best way to help him to learn reading and writing is to try to imagine yourself inside his head, learning what he is learning. And the best way of doing that is to say to yourself, "How did *I* learn to read and write?" Not "How was I taught?" but "How did I *learn*? . . ."

Books are magic because they change things ....

I

The magic world of books

Books are magic because they change things. There, in the book, is our own familiar world – children, grownups, animals, houses, cars, trains. And yet it is not the same. The book has taken these things and transformed them, so that they inhabit a unique and enchanted world, which exists only between the covers of that particular book, and nowhere else. Everything inside the book is part of the magic – the pictures, the characters, the story, even the look of the print and the smell and feel of the paper.

This magic world of books is the world of childhood. It is the birthright of every single child. If you are a parent, one of the most breathtaking and exciting things you can do for your child is to give her the keys of this kingdom.

Like all magic, it is as easy as breathing. Open the covers with a satisfying creak and start turning the pages together, and it is there all around you.

Books begin with stories. The art of the story teller, from time immemorial, has been, as the name implies, in the telling – in the talking. So begin with talking: talk about the pictures as you wander through the book, and tell your child the story that goes with the pictures. How old? One and a half is not too soon to begin, and fourteen is not too old to discover the illuminating power of illustrations in a book, with a trusted friend.

Although sharing books with another human being has no age limit, we'll suppose that you are beginning at the beginning, with a very young child. (If your child is considerably older, simply adapt what you do, and the books you both choose, to suit her likes and interests. This is the beauty of the apprenticeship approach – you can begin with any traveller with any book.)

After a while, when looking at books and listening to stories has become a much loved custom, you can take the tremendously powerful step of moving on from telling to reading. It is a powerful step because now the book itself is taking charge, creating its own world for your child by speaking to her in its own voice and language. You become simply its servant, exploring that world together with your child, in the words of the book itself. It can be a book that is already familiar, or it could be brand new, it doesn't matter. A familiar book is a good idea because then your child suddenly realizes how the magic works. There are black shapes on white paper that are *words*, book words, and these strange new words tell the story of the book in their own special way.

Make the magic easy for her. Point to the words as you go along and link them up with the pictures. Although you don't want to interrupt the magic too often, you can sometimes stop to relish a particular word. "That's a funny looking object, isn't it? Haven't we seen it before, a few pages back? – where was it? Oh yes, there it is, 'Marmalade'. It's a good name for a cat, isn't it – why didn't we think of that?" And the ability to recognize words – to notice that a word is the same as one that has been seen before, the same as an image of that word recorded inside the head – takes root, and begins to grow and flourish.

What is happening is that your child has begun to read.

II

What is happening when your child reads?

Reading is not what we think it is. Real reading happens inside the head.

Many people think that only spoken language is 'real' language. Written words, they declare, are merely a 'code' for spoken language, and a child who is learning to read is learning to 'crack the code' – that is, to say written words aloud. If a child cannot say a written word, according to them, she cannot possibly read it.

On the face of it, this seems like simple common sense. Of course we cannot read words we cannot say.

Or can we? As we investigate this statement, it shifts its ground, and blurs around the edges. For the fact of the matter is quite the opposite – human beings happily and frequently understand words they cannot say. Babies, of course, understand hundreds of spoken words, long before they can say them. But this happens with written words as well. Profoundly deaf children can be taught to understand print, without any reference to spoken language. Hearing children, too, have been taught to read 'non orally' – their teachers gave no indication that written words could ever be matched with speech.[1] Both deaf and hearing children seem to have little difficulty in learning to understand print in this way. And all fluent readers learn the meanings of many new words by reading them, rather than by hearing them. This is evident if they have also learned phonic analysis, and mispronounce new, 'irregular' words, while using them correctly. For example, my daughter informed her father one day that she didn't think he would look very nice with a 'mowst-ake' (moustache)!

If Helen was matching the written word 'moustache' with the wrong spoken word, how did it succeed in conveying its meaning so clearly? Never in any language had she heard this strange pattern of sounds 'mowst-ake', which was original with her; yet when she looked at the written word, the meaning unmistakably came through it.

The reason is that the meaning of a written word *inheres in the shapes*. It is a function, quite simply, of the way the word looks – of its total pattern, the relationship between the various parts, fused into one. The pattern of shapes 'chair' represents of the idea of 'chairness' in a way that the pattern 'chere' does not. Both words can be matched with the identical pattern of sounds. But only 'chair' has been associated for us with that idea in all the books we have ever read. So the word 'chair' has a clear meaning, 'chere' has none. (Unless we're bilingual and also read French, when it has an entirely different connotation.)

Learning to read, then, is not a matter of 'learning to say written words aloud'. Real reading is a process of associating meanings with patterns of shapes. It is silent, unmeasurable, unobservable and invisible. But it happens just as definitely as the process of associating meanings with patterns of sounds, which is also an unmeasurable and invisible process, and babies learn to do it before they are one year old. We call it hearing . . .

Seeing that reading, like hearing, is an understanding process, means that it is worth investigating the process a little more closely. How does it work? How does it begin? Why do we start paying attention to words, so as to learn to understand them? A great deal has been written about how children learn to talk. Very rarely, however, do we discuss the process that has to happen first, the process of learning to *hear*.

For at the very beginning of understanding, there is a paradox. As with many simple and straightforward procedures, learning to hear is logically impossible. In order to learn the meaning of a spoken word, you have to pay attention to it. And what on earth impels you to pay attention to a pattern of sounds, before it has assumed a meaning? Hearing is therefore a non starter, and no one has ever learned to do it.

Oh very well, perhaps we have to think again. Why *do* we pay attention to a word we cannot understand?

Let's suppose that a child is beginning to take note of the spoken word 'chair'. Her mum comes home, and with a sigh and a cup of tea sinks into an armchair. Her dad leaves his glasses on the rocking chair, and the dog sits on them. When it's time for her to have her meals with everybody else, she graduates from her high chair to a proper dining chair.

The interesting thing about all these chairs is that they are really quite different from each other.

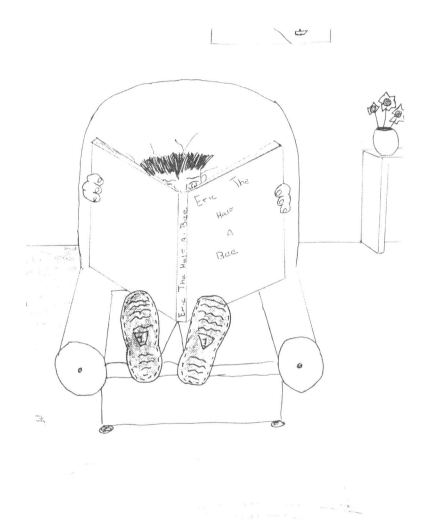

Real reading is silent, unmeasurable, unobservable and invisible ......

A plump and squashy arm chair bears little resemblance to a lean and portable dining chair. And yet each of the objects is labelled with a pattern of sounds that is in every case the *same*.

The child finds this intriguing. Why is the pattern of sounds always the same? And she starts to notice the similar features of these different objects, so as to identify the common factors of 'chairness'. All 'chairs', she observes, have a seat designed for only one sitter, they have some sort of a base which rests on the floor, and they have a back for leaning against. If one of these 'factors' is missing, a back for instance, then whatever-it-is might still be sat upon, but is not a 'chair' and has to be given another name instead.

How old is this child? She may be less than one – she is almost certainly less than two.

And yet, without instruction of any kind, she has just engaged in one of the most formidably intellectual processes available to the human mind. The process is at once highly abstract and passionately creative. Never mind that each separate chair is particular and tangible. The child's concept of 'chairness' is *abstracted* from her awareness of all the different chairs in her experience. It is not a thing at all. It is an idea in her head, and she has created it herself.

The word 'factor' is no coincidence. For the processes at the heart of language are profoundly mathematical. When we learn to understand nouns we are using the self same processes that mathematicians use to identify the highest common factors and the lowest common multiples of sets of numbers.[2] The child is thinking rationally from the very beginning – and that word also is no coincidence. Once she has formed the idea of 'chairness', she can identify a minute doll's chair or a throne in a giant's castle as precisely similar examples of her idea. For the chair, she knows, increases in proportion – in direct mathematical *ratio* – to the size of the sitter . . .

How can we ever have the impertinence to question the intelligence of such a child? Of *course* she is intelligent – brimming over with it – of that there can be no doubt.

And creative too. The child constructs her own meanings. No one else can make them for her. Understanding language is not a passive process, but an active one. The child recreates the world afresh in her own mind, as all her ancestors have done before her, and all her descendants will do after her.

When she has made her meaning, it inhabits the pattern of sounds which first directed her to a discovery of 'chairness'. So now, when she thinks of chairs, she thinks of the word; and when she hears the word, she thinks of chairs. She brings her meaning, freshly made and growing, and grafts it seamlessly on to the pattern of sounds which has become a word.

If she can do all this with a pattern of sounds, why should she not also be able to do it with a pattern of shapes?

Footnotes

1. See James E. McDade, 'A Hypothesis for Non Oral Reading', *The Journal of Educational Research*. Washington D.C.: Heldref Publications, 1937.

2. See Seton Pollock, *The Basic Colour Factor Guide*, p.214.

Learning to read aloud

Reading, and saying written words aloud, are not the same thing. They can happen at the same time, but they may not, and they don't have to. Far from silent reading being a much later achievement, it is the natural first response to print, and the reading out loud which comes second. Later still, when all the associations have been made, the child returns to silent reading.

So should a child be encouraged to read aloud, if it isn't strictly necessary? Naturally she should – it is fun and satisfying to do, and convinces adults that she can 'really read'. More to the point, it convinces the *child* that she can 'really read'. It is a magical process in its own right: the child becomes aware that she has the power to turn these silent black shapes *into sounds*. The sounds are equivalent, and convey the same meanings as the patterns of shapes; they tally, one to one. What a discovery. A child will spend minutes on end working the transformation, and as she does so, the meanings of the written words become clearer and clearer, more and more immediate.

Being able to read aloud accurately also has a great deal to do with accurate spelling, so will pay dividends in the later stages of literacy. It is a good idea to have a bird's eye view of the whole journey before your child even begins, and then you can lay solid foundations for what is to come.

There are all sorts of different ways of helping a child to say written words aloud. The best and most natural is the apprenticeship approach – you do it for her to begin with. Point out words all over the place, and tell her what they say. Relish words you have both noticed as you read a favourite story aloud. "Can you find the word 'dragon' that we read?" (Not, "What is this word?") "Oh, spot on, well done; and there it is again, look." Encourage her to take her turn reading a well loved story to you –

single words, then sentences, then paragraphs, then pages. Help her when she gets stuck, but give her space to think about the tricky words, and have a go at them on her own. Always praise her efforts, and recognize her successes, never her 'failures'. (How can she 'fail'? She is learning all the time.) "That's very good – you got the right meaning, so you could see it in the word. It doesn't *say* 'plate', it says 'dish', but that doesn't matter, you'll say 'dish' the next time." Or, "Hey, you're getting that word 'umbrella' perfectly now, aren't you. Haven't you learned it quickly, you were really stuck on it a few minutes ago."

Don't ask her to read aloud something that is unfamiliar, but a passage whose meaning she knows, so she isn't groping for the story, just practising linking print with speech. And remember that it isn't when she is reading aloud that she is truly learning to read, so time spent on this should be brief, in comparison with the time you spend reading to her. That is when the real reading happens; when, with all her senses alert and her mind working at full stretch, she concentrates her entire small being on bringing meaning to print.

IV

Reading strategies

Another paradox. It is because reading is so immediate and transparent that it is such an elusive process. Continually, we have mistaken what it is all about. We have insisted that it is a matter of 'working out the sounds for written words'. Or, if that seems to fall short of the truth, we have decided instead that it consists of noticing clues and making predictions, getting the meaning from the context.

Both these descriptions fall into the same trap. In each case, we have assumed that what the beginning reader is supposed to be doing is learning to *find out* the meanings of the written words. Either she finds out the meaning by matching sounds to the letters. Or she finds out the meaning from the rest of the sentence, by trying to decide what would fit the sense.

But finding out the meanings of written words, however this is achieved, is always one step away from the reading process itself. Reading is not a matter of 'finding out the meanings', but of *associating* those meanings with written words, when we've got them.

In the beginning, there is word recognition. I 're-cognize' the word 'cough', because *I know I have seen it before*. I have recorded an image of the way the word looks, inside my head, and I have associated this mental image with the idea of a noisy chest spasm.

When I see the word 'cough' on the page, it matches with the image in my mind, which is already associated with a meaning. So I associate the seen word with the same meaning, and hence understand it straightaway.

The very first thing, then, that you need to help your child to do, is to see words clearly, as wholes. This is what is happening when you point out individual words, and see if you can find other words that match them. Provided that at the centre of everything there are books, and reading books together, there is no harm at all in isolating particular words, for your child to attend to.

It's an excellent idea to paint the lower half of one wall in her room with blackboard paint, and write striking words there, in thick, bright letters. (Use the kind of printing already familiar from her books – i.e. a's and g's, rather than ɑ's and ɡ's.) If you do this while your child is asleep, she will be enchanted to discover the words waiting for her in the morning. A large vertical expanse of blackboard is ideal not only for helping with reading, but also writing, later on, so is well worth having.

Then, once the shapes of words are taking hold in her mind, your child needs to associate those words directly with meanings. Don't hamper her by making her work out the meanings for herself. When she has learned to love reading, she will master all the strategies there are, and find out the meanings in any way she can.

To begin with, *you* provide the meanings. You are doing this, by reading books to her, pointing to the words, making the print meaningful. Strictly speaking, you are not even 'providing the meanings' then. What is happening is that the spoken words you use summon up in your child's mind the meanings she has already made for those words. These self made meanings she now brings to the printed words, grafting them together in her mind as she has previously grafted sense and sound. Like the process of learning to hear, the silent and invisible process of learning to read is not passive, but intensely active.

When your child has learned to recognize written words, and to associate them with meanings, she has learned to read. All she needs to do from then on is to practise the art, and she will do this for love of it, because there are books she wants to make her own, becoming adept at reading just by reading.

But how does she, now, find out the meanings of new and unfamiliar words?

It is very simple. In fact there is only one way of learning to understand any new written word: the meaning is invariably provided by a context of some kind. The context can be pictorial; or physical (e.g. the word 'hot' can be presented in the context of a hot radiator, fire, kettle or bath); or the context can be the rest of the sentence; or it can be indicated by the matching spoken word, which has itself been learned in a variety of contexts. When a meaningful spoken word is matched with a written word, all its associations become available, at a stroke, for the equivalent

23

written word, and the meaning is thereby transferred from one to the other.

You cannot teach a child how to use the context to find out the meaning. Well you can, but the process is always roundabout and laborious, and usually self defeating. By the time it is mastered, she has forgotten why she ever needed it in the first place.

So often, though, we feel that before she can 'really read', we must teach her phonic analysis; or sit her down to exercises in 'Cloze procedure', which are sentences with gaps, and she has to use the context to fill in the gaps.

The truth is the other way about. Help her to read, and then you can teach her phonic analysis very rapidly and effectively. Help her to read, and she will tackle 'Cloze procedure' exercises just for fun, because they do indeed 'exercise' a skill she has already perfected by exploring books. The strategies cannot be taught, but they can be demonstrated, while you read together. The more help you give her in the early stages of reading, the more quickly she will progress to the point where she needs no help, because she can do it 'all by herself'.

I was working with a backward reader of eleven, whose parents had enthusiastically cottoned on to the idea that the best way of helping was to read real books to her and with her. Claire herself was ablaze with the discovery that this reading business was after all easy and delightful. At every session with Claire and her Mum, I was told, excitedly, about the amazing new words she was now taking in her stride – 'tremendous', 'deceitful', 'unsportsmanlike'! One day, I was reading with her, and she had something very important to explain. "You see Miss, if I don't know a word, I just read the rest of the sentence, and I can get it."

"Oh Claire," I said, "that's marvellous." She had explained the purpose of Cloze procedure in a nutshell. And then – I already knew the answer, but I couldn't resist the question – "Who taught you to do that?" I asked.

She looked at me as if I was a bit daft. "Nobody *taught* me, Miss. I just do it."

V

Barriers, and how to get round them

All children can learn to read, just as all children can learn to hear.

The human mind has evolved through the understanding and use of symbolic language. The mental processes basic to our understanding of language are also basic to most other human activities, and every child possesses all the intelligence she needs to operate them.

When a child has peculiar difficulty in learning to read, it is because there is some kind of barrier in the way. This barrier, as I've just pointed out, is never a lack of intelligence, or something wrong with the child's learning processes – with the *way* in which she learns.

Because the information used by the human brain always arrives by means of one of the senses (seeing, hearing, feeling, smelling, tasting), difficulty in reading is always caused by a sensory deficiency of some kind, or something that has the effect of a sensory deficiency.

For example, a very simple reason for poor reading is that no one has ever read to the child enough. She just hasn't been exposed to enough meaningful written language to learn to understand it. This has the effect of a sensory barrier because she has been cut off from *seeing* enough meaningful print.

If a child has a moderate or severe hearing loss, she will have difficulty learning the meanings for written words by way of spoken words.

If a child has a visual defect of some kind, she is going to have problems with word recognition because she cannot see the words clearly enough to form accurate mental images.

Or, some people have a visualizing peculiarity which causes the recorded mental images of words to muddle themselves up, and appear, in the mind, in jumbles. Nothing seems to go wrong with the words as they are seen on the page. But because the mental images of words go haywire, word recognition is an uphill struggle. This condition also has the effect of a sensory barrier because it gets in the way of 'inner seeing': it is commonly known as dyslexia.

Now we have identified the real problems, we can see how to tackle them. The thing to do with barriers is to remove them if at all possible. If you can't break them down, then you must get round them, over the top of them or underneath, or bulldoze a way through them. They are never as impregnable as they appear, and there is always a way through somehow. Our job, as parents and teachers, is to find it.

a) *Deafness*

Tackling this problem has to be described as 'breaking the sound barrier'!

Of course there are many different physical reasons for hearing impairment. Most hearing loss is partial: it is rare, nowadays, for a person to be totally deaf. Unfortunately this fact hasn't helped us in our attempt to work out ways of teaching deaf children to read. In Britain at least our teaching methods focus on the restoration of as much hearing as possible, and then using whatever hearing is present to teach the child to read.

This is where an appreciation of the workings of language is vital. Once we have clearly distinguished, in our own minds, between understanding print, and saying written words aloud, we can see how we have been going wrong.

Let's review the facts, from the point of view of a child who is totally deaf. She cannot understand heard words, because she cannot hear them. So her brain cannot get hold of information in that particular way. But she can still *see* words, if they are presented to her, in all their clarity. The effect of her hearing lack is simply that we cannot make those words meaningful to her *by way of spoken words*.

The other three sources of contextual information, however, are still readily available. That is, we can use a pictorial context, or a physical context, or once she has got going with reading, the rest of the sentence can function as a context for an unfamiliar word.

And that is more than enough for anybody.

Exploring picture books is important for a hearing child. For a deaf child, it is a life line. Share as many picture books with her as you can, pointing to the words that go with the pictures. Stick labels on objects around the house, and gradually string words together on her blackboard to form phrases and sentences. If you always point to a sentence in the conventional left to right order, she will soon learn that that is the way to follow the print. Use the same word in as many different contexts as possible – this enables her to eliminate the unlikely meanings, and narrow down to the correct one:

E.g. red shoes, red dress, red ball, red book; three mice, three children, three circles, three bottles.

Think about how a hearing child learns to hear, and try to expose her to written language in the same sort of way. You can't explain or show the meanings of words like 'the', 'and', 'if', 'when' – but keep on presenting them in a meaningful context, and she will learn to understand them.

Above all, don't feel that she has to demonstrate her understanding of print before you introduce new words! This is just what we don't do when a child is learning to hear, which is why the process happens so naturally and rapidly, without stress or strain. The more meaningful written language she sees, the more she will learn to understand, and even if some words are unclear for days or weeks, if she goes on seeing them in all sorts of contexts, they will eventually assume their proper meanings.

At what age can you begin helping a deaf child to understand print? From the very first moment you know she is deaf; ideally begin at the age when a hearing baby is learning to understand speech. That is five months, or less.

For what is happening is that your child is understanding language in exactly the same way as a hearing child. The only difference is that the language she perceives is made of patterns of shapes, instead of patterns of sounds. Seen words rather than heard words will become her basic point of reference, and this makes sense because seen words for her are distinct and detailed, whereas spoken words are not. But once she has learned to understand written language, you can relate other forms of language to print, and help to make them meaningful too. When you are reading books with her, you should say the words to her just as you would with a hearing child, so she begins to link the movements of your lips with the words on the page. Help her to feel the sound of your voice by putting her fingers on your throat when you are talking, to show her that something important is going on inside there. (This discovery will bear fruit when she is learning to speak herself.) If her hearing loss is only partial, the blurred sounds she hears when you are reading to her will gain meanings much more readily if she can relate them to the clear and familiar written words she already understands.

Once again, we must start looking at things 'the other way round'. Instead of feeling that a child's deafness is going to make it difficult for her to learn to read, we must teach her to read because this can help her to hear.

In Book Two of this series, I will try to show that it can also help her to talk.

b) *Visual defects*

The thing to do with this barrier is to break it down if at all possible – that is to compensate by means of special lenses of one kind or another, so that the child can see the print clearly. As with hearing, there are various ways in which vision can be impaired, not all of them apparent from conventional eye tests. If you have any reason to suspect that your child is having sight problems, take her to a qualified ophthalmologist and describe her symptoms carefully and in detail.

Here are some causes of difficulty which may not be identified in the normal course of events. Conventional eye tests are performed on each eye independently. Some children, though, have to struggle to make their eyes work properly together, particularly when they are concentrating on objects close to their eyes like the printed page. After a time, the effort involved causes double images or blurring. Glasses can be prescribed which correct this defect. Any child who complains of headaches or blurred vision after she has been reading for a while should be referred to an ophthalmologist for more detailed tests.

Another problem is lack of a dominant or 'fixed reference' eye. Uncontrolled movements of the eyes make it impossible for a child to make reliable associations between what her eyes are seeing and where they are pointing. The 'Dunlop Test' has been devised to determine whether or not this is happening, and is carried out at the Royal Berkshire Hospital. Treatment is simple: the left eye is occluded. (i.e. the child wears glasses for reading with one lens blanked out). The test must be carried out first, before such glasses are worn, as they will only aggravate difficulties which have a different cause. Contact this address for advice:

The Senior Orthoptist, Royal Berkshire Hospital, London Road, Reading, Berkshire, RGl 5AN. Telephone: Reading 875111.

Visual defects, and true dyslexia (see below), can have similar results as far as literacy is concerned. Advances in this field are frequently made. Coloured lenses, or different coloured print on different coloured paper, can sometimes made a dramatic difference. If you think a change of colour might help, write for details of 'tint testing' to the Irlen Institute, 43 Harrington Gardens, London SW7. Telephone: 01-373-7282. (And see Section VIII in this booklet, on **Choosing books,** which includes suggestions for doing something about the possibility yourself.) Also contact the British Dyslexia Association for up to date information. The address is: The British Dyslexia Association, 98 London Road, Reading, Berkshire, RG1 5AU. Telephone: 0734 668271.

If it is not possible to break down the barrier – that is, if your child's vision is so seriously impaired that she is virtually blind – then you have to get round it, and enable her to read by means of the alternative sense of touch. There are various systems of embossed type. Braille is not the only one, but its advantage is that it can be written by blind people, as well as read. It is based on six dots, like the design on a domino, and consists of sixty three signs made up of all the possible variations of these dots. Twenty six signs represent the letters of the alphabet, and ten more, punctuation marks. They can be used simply to produce a letter by letter copy of print. This is Grade 1 or uncontracted braille, but it is seldom used as it takes up a lot of space and is comparatively slow to read. Grade 2 braille was developed to reduce the size of books and make reading quicker. Other signs are used to represent common letter combinations, e.g. 'ow', 'er', and words such as 'and' and 'for'. Combinations of two signs are also used to represent some words, e.g. 'through'. Some characters may change their meaning depending on how they are spaced.

Just as you would for a sighted child, keep in mind that what your child is learning to read is *language*, and not merely a code for speech.

Concentrate on helping her to read Grade 2 braille as early as possible, concentrate on making the words meaningful, and concentrate on exposing her to a great deal of 'felt' language, rather than just a bit. The intellectual process of 'bringing meaning to print' is the same whether the print is seen or felt, and it really is as easy as hearing. The difficulties are all on the adult's part, in physically making the felt words available and providing the meanings. Getting round that particular barrier is up to you!

Another system of embossed type which is currently used is Moon, a system made up of lines and curves similar to the conventional letters. This is more appropriate for people who lose their sight when they are old, and who may find braille too difficult to master. Its disadvantage is that it cannot be written by blind people themselves, only read, so do not use it with a young child. The address to write to for information is: The Royal National Institute for the Blind, 224 Great Portland Street, London W1N 6AA. Telephone: 01-388-1266.

One or two children, like Helen Keller, are both blind and deaf. The triumph of Anne Sullivan's teaching was that she allowed no barriers to stand in her way. She gave the whole world to Helen Keller by means of the single sense of touch.[3]

c) *Dyslexia*

Realizing that there is nothing wrong with the way any child learns, forces us to the conclusion that dyslexia has to be a perceptual problem of some kind. The only explanation that makes sense to me – and also to the families that I work with – was provided by S.T. Orton in 1937.[4]

The brain is divided into two hemispheres, and the left side of the brain is the 'language centre', where most words are recorded. But certain aspects of language are recorded in the right hemisphere, and when this happens with written words, they are the mirror image of their counterparts registered on the left. Most normal[5] children succeed in blocking out the images, or 'engrams', that are recorded in the right side of the brain, when they are learning to read and write. *But a dyslexic child doesn't.* So sometimes she visualizes the word the right way round. Sometimes she visualizes the mirror image. And sometimes the two images merge and overlap, so she visualizes bits of the word the right way round, while one end snakes back on itself, and turns up in the middle, back to front! Or it rolls itself over, from top to bottom. Or it can do both at the same time, neatly transposing 'p's into 'd's, 'y's into 'h's, 'm's into 'w's.

It is the visualizing process that is playing tricks. Words on the page seem to behave themselves beautifully. The words recorded in the child's mind persist in rearranging themselves in horrendous muddles, so 'apple' can appear as 'alepp', 'abbel', 'pelap', 'plead' – or 'apple', of course, but she has no way of knowing that that is the correct version.

Clearly she is not going to go a bundle on word recognition. The word in front of her sits there in all innocence, looking just the same as it does to everybody else. But there may be no matching version available in her head at that particular moment, so she simply cannot tell you what it says.

The situation sounds desperate, and many dyslexic children do indeed have acute difficulty in learning to read. But it isn't, in fact, nearly as desperate as it seems. Once again, the way of breaking through the barrier is to adopt the apprenticeship approach, and read to a dyslexic child for all you are worth, holding the book so she can see the print, and pointing to the words as you go along.

What happens then is that she gradually learns to assign *any* arrangement of the 'apple' letters to the idea of 'appleness' in her mind. 'Apple' means 'apple' – and so does 'alepp', 'abbel', 'plead', and all the rest. Instead of a single clear image, she forms a cluster of images, which are all permutations of the original word, and whose nucleus is the common meaning. So now, when she sees the word 'apple', she associates it with this cluster, and understands it straightaway. Because the meaning she brings to the word is also associated with the spoken word 'apple', she can usually say the word aloud correctly as well. But she may not – she may look at 'apple' and say 'fruit', 'dish' and say 'plate', 'sofa' and say 'couch'. Dyslexic children commonly find silent reading much easier than reading aloud, and this is one of the indications that can alert you to suspect the condition.

Even though reading aloud is difficult, you should still encourage a dyslexic child to spend some time practising it. Give her all the help she needs, so that she never finds the process threatening. When she gets stuck, don't say, "Oh you knew that word yesterday – think!" Don't try to make her 'work it out'. Give her a second or two to see if it comes, and then tell her the meaning. She should repeat it correctly, and continue. If she baulks at the same word further on, you can point out where it first appeared, and see if that reminds her. But if she draws a blank again, tell her the meaning again. Teachers and parents sometimes wail, "What do you do if a child *cannot* learn a particular word?" and the answer is very simple. You keep on telling her.

Making the distinction between real, silent reading, and 'saying written words aloud', is absolutely crucial when we are working with dyslexic children. Because 'saying written words aloud' feels to us like 'real reading' – because the simultaneity of both processes is so familiar to us – because it is so difficult for us to appreciate the huge difference between 'seeing the meaning', and translating a written word into sounds – we just assume that learning to read is a matter of performance. A child cannot read a book until she can pronounce every word in it correctly.

This is why we think that a struggling reader has to begin with 'easy' reading material. If she is still struggling when she arrives at secondary school, she must stay with the security of a structured reading scheme. Only in this way can she progress. But one reason that reading is so painful for dyslexic children is not that the material we give them to read is too difficult. It is much too easy. Their spoken vocabularies, and their interest level, are often advanced, even beyond their years. The sort of mindless pap we give them to read is excruciatingly boring. Even the well intentioned, simplified material, got up to look like 'real books', is barren fare.

The solution is staring us in the face. All we have to do is to find books that match their interest level, match and extend their spoken vocabularies. And all they have to do is sit and follow the print silently, while we read to them. Because such an activity is so easy and delightful, and doesn't feel like 'work' at all, it takes courage to do it, particularly for the first time. We may spend half an hour just reading to a child, and she may seem not to respond overtly in any way. How can we possibly suppose that she has 'learned' anything?

Screw your courage to the sticking place, and try it, and the children themselves will convince you that it works. You will feel their involvement with the book as you read it to them – grins, chuckles and comments are the real indicators of learning. Next, they will gather confidence in 'reading back' (see p.57). And then their own independent reading will sweep in on the flood tide, often taking both of you by surprise.

I identify incoming strugglers now on the basis of a spelling test, assuming that if they have reading problems they will inevitably find spelling difficult: this screening net trawls for both areas of weakness at once. But I always begin with reading, wherever the specific weakness seems to be. Most poor spellers dislike reading, even if they can 'do' it reasonably well. So my first task is to find a book they will not be able to resist. One little girl stared longingly at a display of Frank Muir's *What-A-Mess* books. "Oh Sonia, try one of those, I'm sure you will like it." She didn't even pick one up, but shook her head. "No Miss, I couldn't, the words are too difficult." "Shall I tell you a secret, Sonia, you have such an amazing mind that it can already read every word in that book, even though you don't know it. Look, I'll show you. I'll read you the book, and all you have to do is to follow the print while I'm reading. Then you can read a bit of it back to me, and you'll be able to do it beautifully. Come on, let's try."

She allowed herself a tiny smile, but still looked puzzled. Didn't I know that reading lessons were supposed to hurt? Disbelieving, she settled herself down next to me, and gradually relaxed into the story of *What-A-Mess the Good*, whose attempts at goodness turned out so disastrously wrong. A few chortles of pleasure, and a small finger pointing in glee to some of the more outrageous illustrations, were all the response I wanted, to begin with. Then it was her turn. We found a bit we had both enjoyed, I re-read just that page to her, and she was launched. She stuck on maybe two or three words, but by the end of the page there could be no doubt that she was reading on her own. The smile, still disbelieving, grew bigger.

"There you are, Sonia, what did I tell you? O course you can read it. I tell you what, if you take this book home with you, I bet you can read it all the way through again. Bring it back next week, and you can have another one. What do you say?"

The smile was definitely a grin as *What-A-Mess the Good* was placed lovingly in her school bag. But the next morning I was hardly out of my car before I was besieged by a small Sonia quite pop-eyed and breathless, jumping up and down with excitement. "Miss, Miss, *Miss*. I read the whole book. All the way through. Last night. By myself!" The last few words nearly disappeared in a squeak. "When can I have another one?"

"Oh Sonia, I told you you could. Isn't that marvellous. Nip into my room after registration and change the book before your first lesson. We won't be able to stop you now, will we?"

Even though the episode had seemed magical to both of us, of course I hadn't waved a wand and mysteriously transformed a non reader into a reader in the wink of an eye. What I had said to Sonia was the truth. She *could* already read, she just didn't know it. All I had given her was the feeling of reading, and the confidence to explore books, by herself. She still needed support. She needed a guide to lead her into new books and different authors, until she had sufficient experience to tackle unfamiliar books on her own. But she knew now that she could do it.

Eleven year old boys who struggle with reading often thrive when they are plunged into *The Hobbit* straight away. We have the sumptuous version with illustrations by Michael Hague, and cheaper copies of the paperback for taking home. What enchants them to begin with is just the thought of reading such a magnificent book. Gradually the story itself takes hold, and they not only re-read the bits I have read to them in class, but keep going almost without noticing, so that when I see them next they can tell me all about the goblins, or the finding of the ring, or the battle with the spiders.

I didn't have the courage to start Edward on *The Hobbit*, though. That was three years ago, and he came in with totally indecipherable writing, and a reading age of six. He also had an amazing spoken vocabulary, and not surprisingly didn't like school. He was often away with minor ailments which had a habit of extending themselves. Just as I felt we were beginning to forge ahead, I wouldn't see him for weeks, and all the ground covered would be lost. Although he dictated some marvellously imaginative work to me, and we had dabbled in several books, by the end of the second year I couldn't pretend that we had cracked the reading. Somewhat diffidently I asked if he would mind a few home visits during the holidays. Then at least I could be sure of reading with him quite often.

Edward didn't mind, and we began *The Midnight Adventure*, by Raymond Briggs – a perfectly ordinary paperback, but short, fast moving, illustrated in black and white, good sized print, and an easy read. I did most of the reading, Edward re-read a couple of paragraphs aloud, and I took the book home with me until the next time. (Like many dyslexics Edward had a positive talent for losing books.) But when we'd finished, I pointed out to Edward that as he had read the whole book, it now belonged to him, and I would give it to him to keep on condition that he re-read it by himself. Edward was quite taken with this idea, so I presented him with the next book in advance. "Then you can re-read it as we go along." (After all, it couldn't stray far.) This was *Charlie and the Chocolate Factory*, by Roald Dahl. Steadily, now, things began to happen. I would arrive and ask Edward to tell me about what he'd re-read, before we started. "Where did we get to, Edward?" I said once, early on into the book. "Here, Miss," he declared, finding the page straight away. There was a small pause; I felt an undercurrent of excitement in the air. Then, triumphantly, "But *I* have got to here," turning over a flurry of pages, and trying not to grin as he looked up at me. "Oh Edward, that's amazing, that's a whole chapter, tell me about it." So he did.

This took us into the Autumn term, and as the home visits were now well established, I carried on with them, once a week. I arrived on one Friday evening feeling disheartened. Edward had been away for the best part of a fortnight, and I was certain he wasn't ill. I knew he wasn't coping with his mainstream work, I knew he needed massive support, and that even with all my efforts I wasn't getting enough going for him in time. Maybe school had finally demoralized him, and he was giving up.

Edward seemed very far from giving up, however: positively cheerful was more like it. "I have something to tell you, Miss," he declared, jigging about on the doorstep. We had barely settled ourselves before he produced *The BFG* (Roald Dahl), his latest book. "Guess how much of this book I have left to read!" "I don't know, Edward, how much?" Keeping his eyes on me, he pinched the last three quarters of the book, waiting for my reaction. But he couldn't suppress a grin. "*Not* this much." He pinched a quarter. "*Not* this much." I gaped. He held just the final page between his thumb and forefinger "*This* much!"

I was literally dumbfounded, and didn't know what to say. At last I found my voice. "But Edward, that's amazing, you only started it two weeks ago. Tell me about it." So he did: Sophie being kidnapped by the Big

Friendly Giant, all the other horrible giants, collecting the dreams, visiting the Queen, and the final rout of the man eaters. The Queen, he informed me, lived in the House of Commons, but he was quite happy to alter this to Buckingham Palace when I explained. "I knew it was somewhere important, Miss."

"Well," I said, still feeling dazed, "you've done so much reading you probably deserve a rest. Shall I read you that last final page, to celebrate?" "Oh yes Miss, please." We finished the book, and then, as usual, I asked him to read back a couple of paragraphs. Once again I felt the prickles going down my spine. *Edward still couldn't read aloud.* Every fourth or fifth word was a battle, even though I had read the page to him just before. If I had asked him to read it 'cold' he wouldn't have been able to manage it at all. The weird thing was that we had done a fair amount of work on phonics, and when I asked him to 'tally' a word (my description of matching sounds to letters), he could do that quite easily. But it clearly didn't occur to him to use the procedure when he was reading on his own.

He volunteered the information that there was a part in the middle of the book he'd had trouble with: "This bit, Miss." It was all in capital letters, and consisted of the descriptions written by the BFG on his bottles of dreams. Just as easy as the rest of the book to translate into sounds, but the patterns of the words were unfamiliar. So naturally Edward couldn't read them. I read him those bits as well, doing some market research on my own account. Did Edward agree with Roald Dahl's ideas about the sort of dreams that appealed to boys and girls? (R.D. will be pleased to know that Edward agrees entirely: he thinks the girls' dreams are wishy washy, but the boys' dreams are brill. As a matter of fact I've had the same sort of comments, but in reverse, from girls. Maybe Roald Dahl knows a thing or two.)

Why such a discrepancy between Edward's silent reading, and his ability to read aloud? What is actually going on in his head when he absorbs a book like *The BFG*, as he clearly does, and with pleasure?

One way of describing it could be that Edward is reading in much the same way that a totally deaf person reads. When he looks at words he sees them as wholes, and he sees the meanings inherent in the shapes. The meanings of some words are clear and distinct, while others are not so sharp; but the more he reads, the more meaningful they become. As his spelling is bizarre, he must be forming a variety of mental images of words, and the business of his mind, while he experiences reading, is a continual grouping of those mental images into clusters which share a common meaning. So intent is he on this that if he is asked to read aloud, it is quite a shock, like shifting into a different mode. Another analogy would be reading and understanding French, and then expressing the sense of it in English. You don't go for an exact, literal translation, but a complete re-thinking in a different language. When Edward sees the words 'Buckingham Palace', of course he sees the same shapes that I see, and he also sees their meaning: an important place in London where the Queen lives. But the fact that the Queen's home is Buckingham Palace (spoken) isn't yet a part of his general knowledge. So he searches his mind for the name of an important place in London where V.I.P.s gather, and comes up with 'House of Commons'. It's quite brilliant, when you think about it.

Brilliant or not, I've been asked by a concerned form teacher to check up on Edward's latest run of absence. "Why have you been away all this time, Edward, what's been the matter with you?" Because I'm in his home, he pays me the compliment of forgetting that I'm One of Them, and instead regards me as an ally. It doesn't occur to him to lie. "Nothing's been the matter Miss, I just stayed away." "But you can't do that, Edward," I say crossly, trying to hold on to a few vestiges of authority. "What have you been doing?" Edward is far too polite to bewail my stupidity, but you can tell that he feels he is underlining the obvious. "I've been reading *The BFG*, Miss," he tells me in surprise, as if that is reason enough. "Oh and on Thursday I went to the hospital for a check up." He has a hole in his heart, so I explain that hospital visits are qute legitimate. It's just that we would like to know. "And I've been reading some easy books to Robert." Edward's older sister, Sarah, is also dyslexic, so it's likely that Baby Robert will be as well. He needs huge amounts of reading input if he is to avoid the sort of problems at school that his brother and sister have experienced. Edward has been taking time out from school, and reading to the baby. Not for the first time, I am at a loss for words. I make an effort. "Yes Edward – but you can't just stay home whenever you feel like it, it's against the law." "I don't see why, Miss, I'm learning far more at home."

He isn't trying to score debating points. Once again he is merely stating the obvious. He would never have read *The BFG* so quickly if he'd kept having to put it down for a science lesson, or a humanities lesson, or anything else that They had decreed was on his menu for the day.

The trouble with me is that I know Edward is speaking the truth. Flashes from my own childhood swim into my mind's eye. The little girl, wheezing her way through still another chest infection, propped up in bed for weeks on end. Seemingly imprisoned in a narrow room at the top of the house, but not really there at all: wandering in Camelot, Sherwood Forest, or the land at the top of the Far Away Tree. Books made my childhood golden. I missed out on many of the scrambling things that healthy children were doing all the time – but I did have books, and my own stories and poems that I tapped out with one finger on my father's typewriter. So that when I *was* at school, during the interludes of health when I could be part of the clanging, bustling confusion along with all the other non wheezing children, any subject that came dressed in written language fell into my hands. Far from being behind in such subjects, I was in fact 'ahead'.

I know too that my own daughters learned to read and write so easily, long before they went to school, because I could teach them at home. I could surround them with meaningful written language naturally and informally, in the same sort of abundant way that they were surrounded with speech. They took literacy for granted, as part of the fabric of their lives.

And I know that one reason so many children leave school illiterate is not that teachers are doing a bad job, far from it. It's just that classrooms are appallingly difficult places in which to learn to be literate. Literacy is not really a school subject at all, but a medium of thought and imagination that children need to experience all over the place, and especially at home. Of course they should extend that experience at school, and take possession there of the many areas of knowledge which are legitimately 'school subjects', and best mediated by written words. But it's the children who never practise literacy at home, just for the love of it, who will find the gates of the kingdom barred and locked against them. The whole point of my job, as I see it, is to get that experience of literacy into as many homes as I can, and to work alongside the school system, in companionship with many others, until we can all discover and share the best ways of 'teaching like parents'.

It's still disconcerting, though, to have my own philosophy reflected back to me in the words of a child who's been truanting because he wants to learn to read and write . . .

"Look, Edward," I say at last, "suppose we decide on a couple of afternoons a week when you could stay at home, with the school's approval. We'll choose subjects that you can slot in and out of fairly easily. Then if your mum agrees to take responsibility for you on those afternoons, you could do whatever reading and writing you wanted, and tell me all about it on Friday when I come round to work with you. But you'd have to make sure you were in school all the other times. What do you think?"

Edward's eyes light up at this suggestion, so we troop downstairs and put it to his mum, who is also enthusiastic. It works to an extent: his attendance gradually becomes less patchy, and as the weeks go by, he explores more and more books.

The main thing that Edward was learning was that books belonged to him. He didn't always have to wait, now, for me to get him into a new book. There were some he could experience all by himself. One Tuesday morning Edward turned up for a school session flourishing *A Game of Soldiers*, by Jan Needle. It was a perfectly ordinary paperback about the Falklands war, in small print, with no pictures. "I didn't think you'd mind, Miss, I swiped it from your room on Friday when you were on the top site." He placed it carefully on the bookshelf. "I'm putting it back because I've finished it."

The double take took a while. "Edward! What d'you mean, you've *finished* it?" Edward must often have the feeling that he is explaining things to someone of limited mental capacity. "Well Miss, I started it on Friday, I read it on Saturday and Sunday, I read it yesterday, and I finished it this morning at break time." I registered the 'break time' bit in passing, knowing I would gloat over that later, and took a deep breath. "But that's amazing, Edward, tell me about it." So he did. He hadn't realized that the story concerned the Falklands, but when I explained the background he assimilated it immediately, pointing to the face of the soldier on the cover. "So he's an Argentinian soldier, then, Miss?" Nor could he tell me the names of the three children, though he could easily identify them as an older boy and girl, and a small boy. Clearly when he saw the names in print they conveyed meanings, but not the spoken equivalents. (We respond to names in Russian novels in much the same way.)

Maybe Edward was ready for *The Hobbit*. I told him about the dwarves whose gold had been stolen by Smaug the dragon, and we gazed at the picture of the fearsome beast, spread magnificently across a double page and heaps of gold. At the bottom of the right hand corner was a shadow, tiptoeing its way in. That was the burglar, Bilbo the hobbit, only at the beginning of the story he didn't know he was a burglar, and had no desire to go adventuring. Not until Gandalf came to call did he – but what did Edward think? Would he like to try it? Yes he would, and together we made our way forward, using the pictures as stepping stones to mark our passage. Luckily I managed to find another copy of the illustrated version for Edward to read at home, as I didn't think he could tackle the book in bare print just yet.

It was our most ambitious project so far, and after several chapters Edward decided he needed a breather. I didn't quibble. He knew far better than I where he was going, and how fast he could travel. He tackled *The Machine Gunners* (Robert Westall) instead, but when he was about three quarters of the way through it, he mislaid his copy, and I didn't have a spare one for his school session. There on the window sill across the room from us, however, was the monstrous Smaug, glowering from the front cover of *The Hobbit*. Edward retrieved the book with a sigh of relief, and carried it to the reading corner. "It's all right Miss, we'll read this instead, can we?"

Now there was no holding him. So far I had done most of the reading, but once again, as I arrived at his home on a Friday night, he began responding to my question, "Where have we got to, Edward?" by finding the page, and then, after the usual pause for effect: "But *I* have got to here!" several pages further on. The exciting thing was that neither of us could really believe what was happening. But there it was, he could tell me all about what was on the new pages, so he must be reading them. Once he told me that he'd taken the book with him on a visit to his Dad. "On Sunday afternoon, Miss, we were all watching television, and it was a bit boring, so I went upstairs and read *The Hobbit* instead." He liked the way I was continually astonished. "You did *what*, Edward?" Then he would repeat his explanation with a grin.

It is largely because of Edward that I have now learned to offer *The Hobbit* to my first year reluctant readers. As he says, "It's got lots of difficult words in it, Miss, but it's much more interesting than those little short books." *The Hobbit* is indeed at their interest level, so the reading advances on all fronts to catch up.

Edward and I have cracked the reading simply because I was convinced of the total difference between the two reading processes. I knew it didn't matter if he couldn't read aloud. All the time I was reading to him, and he was sitting beside me, absorbed in following the print, he wasn't 'preparing' to read, or 'learning how' to read. He was having the direct and immediate experience of real reading then and there. That is, he was looking at patterns of shapes and associating them with meanings. He didn't see exactly the same meanings in the words that I saw, because no two people ever do. And to begin with, I imagine, he brushed the words with the merest surface haze of meaning, too fragile and insubstantial to take his unsupported weight. But it was real reading nevertheless; and because I had the faith to go on reading to him indefinitely, the associations grew stronger and stronger, until he discovered, almost without realizing it, that he could experience meaningful print in exactly the same way on his own. I didn't know just when the independent reading was going to begin, and it wasn't important that I should. So the 'performance' had come rolling in, in far greater abundance than if I had been aiming at a specific response at the end of each session.

The lack of concern with the child's performance is the truly liberating factor. Edward needs to be able to read aloud, and he needs to be able to write and spell accurately. Alongside his exploration of the world of books, I am trying to give him experience in those areas as well. But I know that his reading ability doesn't need to mark time while he learns to master the separate skills of matching print with speech, and producing written words himself.

This is why the apprenticeship approach to reading is vastly different from, say, 'paired' reading, or 'shared' reading. Paired reading involves adult and child reading aloud together simultaneously. Transactions of knocks and nudges are used to indicate to the child's partner when she feels able to read aloud by herself, and when she needs help. Shared reading often means that parent and child take it in turns to read aloud. All three approaches are superficially alike in that parents and children are encouraged to read together in a positive way. But only the apprenticeship approach recognizes that real reading is silent reading, and it puts no pressure on the child to perform before she is ready. Children with severe dyslexia can find 'paired' or 'shared' reading frustrating, and parents tell me that the sessions often end in tears, which is a great pity. Apprenticeship reading means that nobody worries about the actual process. All the attention is concentrated on the books, and whether they are a good read or not![6]

It's true that I needed to spend a great deal of time with Edward. I was prepared to invest my own time because I was fascinated by the whole undertaking; however, we can't expect professionals to do this as a matter of course. (Edward's mother is supportive and encouraging, but she is a single parent and her youngest child is a toddler: she has her work cut out just to survive.) The time isn't the real barrier, though. There are word for word cassette tapes, grannies, volunteers and other children, as well as parents and teachers. There is also television, which hasn't even begun to realize its potential as a means of bringing the vivid experience of literacy into every home. Once we see how effective the apprenticeship approach is, we can easily develop ways of providing the necessary reading input, for all children.

No, the real barrier is our own difficulty in imagining what it must be like to read silently, without a continual reference to inner speech. If we stop to think about it, we realize that it has to be possible, because this is how profoundly deaf people read, but it's presumably a bizarre and awkward procedure.

In fact, it is natural and straightforward. The best way of 'catching yourself doing it' is to imagine that you are a small deaf child. You cannot hear, and you cannot speak. But you have learned to understand print. If, for example, somebody shows you this sentence, you can understand it straight away:

The chocolate fudge is in a jar on the top shelf in the kitchen.

When you look at the words, you don't 'see the sounds'. What you see in your mind's eye are pictures: of delicious chocolate fudge, stored in a glass jar, on the top shelf in the kitchen. You can easily demonstrate this perception by dragging a chair into the kitchen, climbing up and standing on tiptoe, and helping yourself.

(Something interesting to notice is that just as the meaning of a word is more than the sum of its parts, so too is the meaning of a sentence. It is an organic whole. Every word affects and is affected by the meaning of every other word. It isn't until you reach the final word 'kitchen' that you know where to take the chair and discover the fudge; but equally, the meaning of 'chocolate fudge' casts its meaning forward, because it is the fudge that makes the kitchen interesting.)

The point is that everyone reads that sentence in just the same way as the deaf child! What springs to mind first is a vision of sweetmeats stored in glass jars. You look through the words and see their meanings. Think of when you are absorbed in a novel: the main concern of your mind is with the mental imagery conjured up by the words. If you want to, you can also slow down and think of their matching sounds, but that is something different.

Now you have a look at another sentence, written in Swahili.

Siku ya kwanza alileta mayai kumi na matano; siku ya pili, kumi na sita; na siku ya tatu, kumi.

(If you can understand Swahili, pretend you can't.) The Swahili written language is totally phonetic, but one or two sound values are different from ours. The letter 'i' is pronounced 'ee', 'ay' is pronounced 'ī', and 'e' is pronounced 'ā'. Armed with this information, you could scrutinize each word and read the whole thing aloud. But if I said to you, "Oh well done, you have read that beautifully," you would give me a disgusted look. "Do me a favour," you would say. "I haven't read it at all. I don't have the remotest idea what it's about."

You are right, you haven't read it. What you have done with it has been valid, satisfying and useful – it just isn't reading. Notice also that the way you look at the two sentences is quite different. When you read the first sentence, you see the words as transparent wholes, and you have the feeling of looking through them. When you tackle the second sentence, your focal point comes sharply forward. Instead of looking through the words, you look at them, much more analytically. Now your concern is to separate each word into bits, so as to match sounds to each bit, and produce an equivalent spoken version.

All children need to be able to look at written words in this careful and analytical manner, as it is a vital foundation for accuracy in writing. (See Book Two, *Saying Written Words Aloud*). But we have to appreciate that it *is* a separate process, and that when our concern is with enjoying books, the silent reading comes first.

Footnotes:

3. See Helen Keller, *The Story of My Life*, 1st ed. 1902.

4. S.T. Orton, *Reading, Writing and Speech Problems in Children*, 1937.

5. In one sense, there is no such creature as a 'normal' child. But I find the word useful to describe children with no sensory 'peculiarities' or defects.

6. However, see P.76 for a variation of paired reading which is easily combined with the apprenticeship approach, and which helps youngsters like Edward to gain the vital practice in reading aloud necessary for spelling.

VI

Working with older children

Teachers and parents also sometimes ask, "When should you stop reading to a child?" and the nicest answer is "Never".

Parents can look quite doubtful when I suggest reading to an older child (twelve, thirteen, fourteen). Isn't she going to feel demeaned? Very often, though, the child looks delighted. This is what she has hungered for, without knowing it – someone who will sit down beside her, and just show her how it is done.

It is true that some children with literacy problems resist, and they have to be wheedled and coaxed into it, just as you would cajole a child hovering on the edge of the pool in her arm bands, not wanting to take the plunge. But once the custom is well established in a family, the children want it to keep going long after they have learned to read independently. Some children even pretend they cannot read by themselves, because they are afraid that Mum will stop reading to them!

For what you are doing is not 'teaching', but exploring books together, getting to know the same characters, gurgling over the same funny bits, sharing the suspense as the action gathers pace. Parents who have wandered the enchanted shores of a well loved book with their child have established a bond that no other experience can give, and through which they can gain a deeper understanding of themselves, of each other, and of the world they both inhabit.

I was working with one eleven year old because he had severe spelling problems, although reading came easily. Nevertheless, he took home my standard letter, about apprenticeship reading, and his parents began to come to sessions with me. His mother explained her reaction to the letter – it had dawned on her, she said, that although Lee *could* read perfectly well, he *didn't*. There was always something else he would find to do instead. I remarked that this was probably because of his visualizing

45

peculiarity, which was causing the difficulty with spelling. The reading hurdle had fallen, because his mother had indeed read to him a great deal when he was younger. But independent reading was still a fairly uncomfortable and awkward process, and he wouldn't do it by choice.

So once again his mother started reading books with him and his younger brother. At a later session she reported gleefully what had happened as they neared the end of *The Iron Man*, by Ted Hughes. "Lee was cheering!" she said in amazement. "He was literally jumping up and down! But then – you are going to like this – we had been so involved that we had hardly noticed my husband was putting up shelves in the same room. Afterwards he said, "You know I was enjoying the book as well. When are you going to read another one?"

Almost by accident, the whole family had stumbled over an activity which gave all of them a great deal of pleasure. It wasn't expensive, they didn't have to drive miles for it, and it wasn't sitting down and watching television!

Few things are more exciting than helping a pre-schooler to fall in love with books, which is what happened for me when my own childen were little. But working with older children is just as fascinating, because very often they can articulate for you what is happening inside their heads. Most of what I know I have learned from children, by asking real questions, like, "Is this how it feels? Does that make sense? Do you think this will help?" When they realize that I do genuinely want to know the answers, they begin to take me into their confidence. It is called 'explaining to Miss'. It has only happened over the past few years, now that I have, at long last, been able to reorganize the Special Education department along apprenticeship lines. Enthusiastically, I try to involve my colleagues, and many are very attracted by the idea. But they still feel that such an individually based approach cannot be operated in a school. "It's too expensive in teacher time," they declare sadly. It isn't: and this is because when we are helping a child to read, we must come to recognize that the teacher is the last resort, and not the first. Let's review in more detail all the other forces available. Parents are in the front line, then come the adult volunteers. Grannies are marvellous, for very often, without giving it a name, they have already used the apprenticeship approach to help two generations of children to read. They also have the time to spare to come into school during the day, when their sons and daughters are at work.

But more than this, our schools are bursting with hundreds of potential teachers who know how to do it because they are passionately and immediately involved in the learning process themselves. They are called children. Children are some of the best teachers there are. A child can explain something to another child in five minutes, when the adult teacher has been struggling to convey it for the whole lesson. The child can pinpoint how the teacher is going wrong, because having just been there herself, she knows exactly what her fellow pupil doesn't understand. In my Special Education room now, we are all teachers, we are all learners. The only difference is that I am a bit older and have a few more wrinkles; also I get paid for it, which is lovely.

So third year pupils stay behind once a fortnight after school, and read with my second years. Fifth years do the same with first years. (The reason for this arrangement is that these are the years which happen to end the day on the same site.) The fifth years are already experienced because last year, when they were fourth years, I worked with two groups on a module called 'Books, Writing and Kids'. We all traipsed over to the primary school and practised on the little ones, reading to them and with them, writing down stories and poems from their dictation, encouraging them to copy out and illustrate their own work, if they were able to and wanted to. The primary school children seemed to relish being guinea pigs, but it was my fourth years who really enthused about the experiment. Many commented in their written reports that it was the module they had most enjoyed, because it had given them practical insight into how easily they could help their own children, when they were parents. Now some of them are keeping their hand in by traversing the same territory with my first years.

The principle we all try to follow, when teaching someone else, is 'Assume total ignorance, and also total sense.' This is not patronizing. As I point out to the children, it is exactly what I need from a teacher, in my role as learner.

For example, I have done a deal with Colin, a second year, who attends Special Education sessions because of his spelling. His spelling may be original, but so is his work on computers: he could happily spend the whole day inventing new and spectacular tasks for the computer to perform.

"Colin," I tell him, "I know nothing – well, virtually nothing – about computers. If I help you with your spelling, will you teach me about computers?" No need to ask twice, but I have to teach him how to teach me. "Colin, remember you are dealing with a computer illiterate here. You are going much too fast – slow down, and explain it bit by bit. Go through that sequence again, and tell me why you are doing it."

Which reminds me – if you are a teacher, and are looking for a good inservice course about teaching reading, you can hardly do better than go on a computer course conducted by experts. You will find out just how a beginning reader feels in the classroom – totally befogged. Another teacher and I decided we had to get to grips with the mysteries of computers, so we could use them more effectively with our 'special' children, and we made the mistake of going to the middle session of what was anyway an intermediate course. Rarely have I experienced anything more dramatic, or more salutary. We had gone quite humbly, hoping to be shown a few discs, what they were designed to teach, and how they did it. Instead, the lecturer conducted an involved and learned discussion about the advantages of something called 'Prolog' over something called 'Basic'. Chris and I were out of our depth straightaway. At the end of the talk we looked at each other in horror, and spoke almost with one voice. "Now I know *exactly* how Edward feels."

The lecturer, quite justifiably, had not been able to assume total ignorance on our part. What she said may have been sensible and helpful, but because we had no way of getting to grips with it, it just washed over our heads.

Now imagine a child with a visualizing difficulty, whose parents, through no fault of their own, have not been able to give her any literacy input – they haven't read books to her or with her, so she has no idea how the print goes, or how delightful books can be. Most children have had this sort of input at home. Their parents, often without realizing it, have already taught them to read. When they get to school, the teacher adds the finishing touches by helping them to 'say written words aloud', which she regards as 'real reading'. But the child who has had no previous experience of books has no way of getting to grips with what is going on in the classroom. She is quite out of her depth, and the teacher doesn't realize she is in desperate need of the nine tenths of input which her classmates have already had – that before ever she can be expected to produce the final tenth of 'output', to 'say written words aloud', someone has got to sit down and just read to her until it is coming out of her ears. She does indeed have the 'total sense' necessary to learn to read. What her teacher must do initially, though, is to assume the 'total ignorance'.

Very often, the hurdles on the way to literacy, faced by a child with a visualizing problem, are piled one on top of another. She not only needs reading input from adults, she needs about five times as much as other children, to get to the same place – because, in effect, she has to learn about five times as many words! Yet her parents may be unable to provide it, because visualizing problems are hereditary, so it is more than likely that one or both of the child's parents suffer in the same way. When she gets to school, the teacher is unaware of the best way of meeting her 'special needs', and expects her to learn to read aloud almost immediately, which is exactly what she finds most difficult. She doesn't know enough to know that she has the sense to do it, if only she is given the input. Her classmates, and possibly her teacher as well, think she is stupid. Perhaps she *is* stupid. And so the frustration, despair and bitterness begin to take hold, and spoil school for her, which should be an exciting place, full of new things to learn and friendly people to learn them with.

Because the road to literacy is the same for all human beings, the first thing to do for any struggling reader is to provide this input, which she hasn't had. She can be two years old, or five, or eleven, or twenty eight.[7] What she needs first is to be exposed to as much meaningful written language as possible. Then she will indeed 'break through' into the discovery that she can understand print independently.

All my eleven year olds have their 'break through' books. For Martyn, it is a 'Gumdrop' book. Martyn came to us as a first year, convinced that he was 'rubbish' at reading. But he enjoyed the books about Gumdrop, the 'Austin Clifton Heavy Twelve-Four, vintage 1926' by Val Biro. He especially liked listening to *Gumdrop has a Birthday,* and after a while, with help, he decided he could read bits of it aloud by himself. Now he can read the whole book aloud, all the way through. His constant litany, while he is reading it to me, is, "Don't say anything, Miss, I can do it." I wouldn't dream of saying anything, as the words which were once so opaque for him fall into place, transparent as glass. He must have read it ten times already, but whenever a new reading partner appears he promptly sits them down to listen, breaking into song for the 'He's a jolly good fellow' and 'Happy birthday to you' bits, and pointing out with a grin that 'Horace *likes* cakes'. For he knows, as his partner doesn't, that Horace the dog is going to make off with Gumdrop's birthday cake, and scoff the lot.

Toby, Martyn's companion in arms, has made *The Favershams*, by Roy Gerrard, his 'break through' book. This is a most unlikely book for a child to latch on to – a series of verses about Charles Faversham, and his progression through the ranks of the British Raj! The illustrations are weird, towering affairs, full of squat little figures at the bottom, disappearing into an infinity of trees and sky, curtains and windows, at the top. Toby loves it passionately, and will read it again and again, to anyone with fifteen minutes to spare. He says simply, "I like that book, Miss," to which we respond, with feeling, "We know, Toby, we know."

Jo is dyslexic. Reading comes easily, but reading aloud is slow and halting, a source of embarrassment. Spelling is worse. To my shame, we didn't even identify her problems until she was in her fourth year, although other teachers had noticed them and had been agitating for something to be done. But she had never been placed in one of my 'remedial' groups. When I was finally able to work with her on her own, I asked her, my heart in my mouth, if she would mind being read to. She had experienced so much patronizing exasperation from the academic system over the years, and I dreaded to seem to be adding to the load.

However, I needn't have worried. Her face broke into my first 'Jo grin'; sheer relief, I think, that I wasn't another teacher waving expectations under her nose. "Oh no," she said reassuringly, putting me at ease. "My mum reads to me all the time."

It was quite true. Flying in the teeth of everything officialdom had told her about learning to read, Jo's mother had read to her daughter ceaselessly, from babyhood on, right into her teens, holding the books so she could see the print, not worrying about whether or not Jo could say the words herself. And Jo had learned to love books, not to be afraid of them. In sheer instinctive desperation, Jo's mother had triumphantly and beautifully taught her daughter to read. That is, the words on the page spoke to her, bright and soundless.

She and I compared notes, and discovered that we shared a similar taste in books. We like the strange and offbeat, books that explored the hidden reaches of the human mind. So we began with Hannah Green's *I Never Promised You a Rose Garden,* which is a superb and compelling account of a young girl's emergence from schizophrenia. In order to escape from a reality too terrible to face, Deborah, the protagonist, flees to a yet more forbidding kingdom of her own devising, with laws and gods and a language all its own. I read the first chapter, and it gripped us both. Jo took the book home and finished it herself. She also borrowed the video and watched that, reporting that it was good and well acted, but not as good as the book! As her confidence grew, she began to read back to me portions of the book that I had already read to her, becoming more and more fluent with each attempt. She knew that if she stumbled I knew why she stumbled, and was there to give her a helping hand across the rocks.

It would have been grossly impertinent of me to suggest that I 'taught Jo to read'. Jo's mother had done that years before. What I was able to give her was far less important, but it helped. It was the conviction that the academic system, after all, did recognize her ability and potential, and acknowledged that what she had already learned to do with books was most definitely reading. Later, Jo gained an 'O' level in English Language. I like to think that I was one of the ones who gave her the confidence that she could do it.

It has taken me a long time to realize the power of illustrations in books for older children. I couldn't use picture books with them, could I – picture books, almost by definition, were for babies, not for my anxious and defensive adolescents. But somehow, willy nilly, I came across them, or the children brought them in themselves, and now my Special Education room is adorned with Raymond Briggs' *Fungus The Bogeyman, Gentleman Jim, Father Christmas, The Snowman;* Maurice Sendak's *Where The Wild Things Are;* Charles Keeping's illustrated version of *The Lady of Shalott.* (Piles of *Tintin* books we have always had.) Michael, a first year, inspects *The Snowman* in amazement. "I can't read this, Miss, there aren't any words." "Oh yes there are, Michael – *they are all inside your head.*" "Oh." And then, as light dawns: "Oh!" And he sits down and murmurs his way through the book, reading with delighted confidence the words that are totally invisible and blazingly real. (Would you believe that I have discovered *fifth* years sneaking into my room after their 'mocks', shamefacedly but avidly devouring *Fungus The Bogeyman* and *The Snowman!*)

Robert's reading was slow and halting when he came to us as a first year. Now, a third year, every book he takes home is a poetry book. He fell in love with Shel Silverstein's *Where the Sidewalk Ends*, and brings it to registration, passing it around to his mates, so they too can relish the sheer impossibility of the drawings. He makes certain to reclaim it when the bell rings – his mates can look, but only he, Robert, may borrow; he is special.

For some children, who have never before experienced the sense of power and glory that possession of a real book confers, the only entrance I can find is through the world of dragons and monsters depicted in the *Fighting Fantasy* game books. I have an uneasy relationship with these books, but I know they appeal to an adolescent's fascination with mock battles and fearsome beasts. Viewing a child who is intensely involved in recording his scores, gold pieces, keys and potions on an adventure sheet, walking tall because *he* is the hero, staking his life on the throw of a die, I cannot bring myself to wall up this particular means of entry. They bulldoze a way in, these books – and then, so long as many others are on offer, they are indeed discarded.

But I have also learned to be wary of them. It was Darrell who taught me that, weighed in the balance of his own fierce morality, they fell short, they did not answer. Darrell was eleven, still stumbling on the outskirts, and a few battles with monsters, I thought, might give him access. We began with *The Warlock of Firetop Mountain*, but I soon realized I was out of my depth when we met our first dragon. "Do you want to fight the dragon, Darrell?" I inquired, rattling our cheerful coloured dice. However, Darrell was very definitely against fighting dragons, and I began to search for the alternative section. "I don't want you to think I'm *afraid* of fighting the dragon, Miss," he said earnestly, stopping me in my tracks. "You see, I'm very fond of animals, and I wouldn't like to hurt it."

That was my first moment of doubt: I had more than a suspicion that making friends with the beast was not going to be the alternative we were offered. Hastily reading the section to myself, in advance, I discovered I was quite right. The alternative was worse. We were going to have to try casting a spell, which would shrivel the dragon to ashes if it was successful. (If it wasn't successful, of course, the dragon was probably going to shrivel Darrell.) "I don't think you'll like this, Darrell," I said hesitantly. "You're going to have to try a magic spell which could shrivel it to bits. It's either fighting it or shrivelling it, I'm afraid."

Darrell took time to think. "I'd better fight it, then," he said. But I was not to be let off lightly. He was moving in a world of his own, and he had to explain his decision. "You see Miss, when its mother and father come to look for it – well, I know it's a grown up dragon, but it will still *have* a mother and father. *My* mother has a mother and father – well, she has a mother and her father – that's my grandfather, Miss – is dead. But my mother is a grown up, you see Miss, so it's the same with dragons – " (I had been wondering if we were going to get back to the dragon) " – so its mother and father will come looking for it. If I've just had a battle and killed it, they'll find its body, but if it's all shrivelled to nothing, they won't. So I'll fight it."

To my enormous relief the bell rang at that moment, and I could cravenly postpone the battle with the dragon until our next session. By then I had found a solution. "I tell you what, Darrell," I suggested, "why don't we just *pretend* you've fought the dragon, and go on to the next bit?" Fortunately, he could accept that idea without any moral qualms. "Oh *yes* Miss," he said at once, breaking into one of his delightful grins. "Then it won't really get hurt."

After that I conveniently mislaid the book, and we began to read *The Lion, the Witch and the Wardrobe* instead. He settled into it with a sigh of recognition, and within weeks he had made it his own.

For Darrell, like all other children, is special. My job is to look and hunt and search until I have found the special book, for every special child, which will lead him into the kingdom.

Footnote

7. The reason the adult literacy movement is so effective is that the tutors work with students on a one-to-one basis – the apprenticeship approach at the other end of the age range!

Dragons are people too.

VII

A step by step guide

Always have a plan.

I plan my Special Education sessions in detail, working out to the minute who is going to be doing what, when and for how long. Generally the plan is abandoned in the first five minutes. Somebody has had yet another brilliant idea, which has to be implemented straightaway, if I would please please *please* allow the time and materials. Or one of the students is away, which means that someone else can have their time on the computer, or their 'input' time with me. Still, the exercise of planning has itself been helpful, and gives an underlying structure to what I am trying to achieve.

When reading with their child is a new departure for a parent, I usually suggest that they arrange a fairly strict timetable together. This is just to ensure that they both approach the undertaking seriously, and go out of their way to establish it as a family custom. Once it is established, they can modify it to suit themselves, and the whole procedure will become much more natural and flexible.

If you like the idea of having a structure to help you, as you venture out into the territory of sharing books with your child, you could begin by negotiating a contract with her. Older children respond positively to this – it makes it all sound grown up and official. In addition, it puts the activity on the right footing from the beginning. Parent and child are going to be involved as equals, with similar obligations to each other; so the child feels that she is being consulted, that her ideas and feelings are being taken into account, and carry as much weight as her partner's. She isn't just having something foisted on her.

Here is the contract we use, deliberately written in posh handwriting and impressive legal sounding language:

Bear in mind that because you are going to be doing most of the 'work', you can have a reading session when your child is ready for bed, just before she goes to sleep. Then it doesn't conflict with activities that happen earlier – time spent with her friends, homework, watching favourite television programmes.

READING CONTRACT

We, the undersigned, agree to spend twenty minutes a day, three days a week, reading together. To begin with, the contract will last for two weeks, but can be renewed as we decide.

Neither party can break this contract without the consent of the other.

The days we have chosen are

——————, —————— and ——————.

Starting date : ——————

Signed : ——————

——————

And here is a copy of the leaflet I give to parents, so that they have a procedure to go by while they are finding their feet:

THE APPRENTICESHIP APPROACH

A Reading Instruction Sheet

1. Help your child to choose a book she really *wants* to read. (A list of suggested books is available.) You can reject her choice if you wish (then you must choose another). But try to go along with it if you can!

2. You should both look for an attractive, enjoyable book, with super illustrations. The book should be a bit *too* difficult for your child to manage on her own. (This is the exciting part.)

3. You read to her for about fifteen minutes. (You may need to read for longer if you are starting a new book, and want to get both of you into it.) *You* do this reading even if her own reading is quite good. You are sharing an enjoyable book together. Hold the book so she can see the print. Encourage her to follow as you read. If necessary run your pencil or finger under the words as you go.

4. Concentrate on *enjoying* what you are reading. Make it as dramatic as you can. Shout or growl for the angry bits. Whisper the frightening bits. Stop and talk about where the story is going if you want. (Or discuss what the material is about, if it's more factual.)

5. When you reach a good stopping place, she reads back to you for about five minutes. She should 'read back' the last couple of paragraphs you have read to her, if possible. If you think she would enjoy a more exciting bit, further back, you can re-read just that part to her. You want the meaning to be really fresh in her mind when she tackles it herself.

6. If she gets stuck on a word, give her about five seconds to think about it – then just tell her what the word says. Don't try to make her 'work it out'. (Don't worry – you will be helping her to 'work out' words later. It's very important not to bother her with all that at the beginning.

Concentrate on enjoying the book.) She should repeat the word correctly, then carry on.

7. Praise her. Say things like, "That was super! That was fantastic! I never thought you were going to get that word right – and you did." Say things like, "Hey, that was incredible! I thought you were supposed to be bad at reading. You are not bad at all – you are *ace*." Whenever she gets a word right that she got stuck on before, say, "Well done! You're learning it. That's excellent."

8. Praise her. (See above.)

9. Praise her. (See above.)

10. (It works!)

I have found that this way of tackling 'reading problems' is invariably effective, so it's worth spending a little time reviewing the key features of the approach, and being clear in your own mind about why it achieves such positive results, so rapidly.

a) You are spending most of the time reading to your child, indicating the print as you go along, making it meaningful. This is when she is really learning to read. You are giving her the experience of following print in an easy, fluent fashion, seeing the meanings in the written words, and enjoying their actual purpose, which is to tell her a story.

b) She spends only a small proportion of time reading aloud to you, so she doesn't feel that reading is always a struggle, a task that she has to 'perform'.

c) When she does read aloud, she is not tackling an unfamiliar passage, but material that you have just read aloud to her. Remember that learning to read is not a matter of finding out the meanings of new words, but of seeing the meanings *in* words. You are showing her that this is something she can do, and that it's fun.

d) She cannot fail. Whenever she gets stuck on a word, you give her a moment or two to see if it comes, and then you tell her the meaning again. You may have to do this four or five times with a particular word. After that, she will have it.

e) You are sharing a real book with her, at her interest level, not the sort of 'easy reading material' which is an insult to her intelligence. 'Easy reading material' doesn't make reading easy, it makes it hard – because your child is never exposed to a rich and interesting vocabulary, so she has no opportunity of learning to read it! As you continue to read together, you will probably be amazed by the long and complicated words that start tripping off her tongue. (Your child will be just as amazed and delighted, and will tackle the whole business with increasing enthusiasm.) It's often the little sneaky words which are the real pests, but they will steadily fall into place as you keep going.

f) The book is at the centre of what you are doing, not the process of learning to read. Learning to read should always be about enjoying books, so the book comes first, second and last. If you're not enjoying a particular book, scrap it and find another one. (Occasionally a book has to be given a chance! If you are very confident about the treasures of an old favourite, keep going for a little while, but if it still doesn't appeal after two or three sessions, give up. You can always come back to it next year.)

As your love affair with books takes off, it is a good idea to keep some kind of record of your journey together. With each of my students, I compile a list of the books they have experienced. This could mean that the entire book has been read to them, or they have followed a book while listening to it on tape, or they have shared the reading with a reading partner, or they have read the whole book themselves. Some books are abandoned half way through: this doesn't matter. But if a book has been completed, in any of the above ways, the child is asked to assess its 'enjoyment factor'. My students have heard of 'good food guides' – this is the 'good book guide'. Of course the only person qualified to know how much she has enjoyed a particular book is the child herself, so she decides whether it is a five star book (the top accolade, as with hotels) or merely a two or one star book.

This sort of record keeping has several advantages. If you maintain it over several years, it is fascinating to look back and see 'the sort of books that really appealed to you two years ago. After that you liked so-and-so's books, and now you are keen on science fiction. I wonder where we'll be going next.' It underlines the idea that the exploration of the world of books is a continual journey, with many exciting countries that can be visited briefly, or where you can linger for months before moving on. Countries previously visited can once again delight the traveller with their familiar landmarks – there is no harm at all in returning to 'easier' books while the child gathers her confidence for the next transition. In fact real books are neither 'easy' or 'hard', but accessible or inaccessible, nourishing or barren.

Another advantage is that while you are definitely making a record of progress, which involves a thoughtful and judicious assessment procedure, *it isn't the child's performance that is being assessed.* On the contrary, it is the child's opinion that is being sought, she is the one who is being deferred to. The books are the objects of scrutiny and evaluation, and this is as it should be. For whether a child becomes a real reader or not never depends on the 'teaching method' being used, or the number of words she learns in a week, or the personality of her teacher, or even the relationship between teacher and child.

It depends simply on the books she reads, and whether she likes them.

VIII

Choosing books

'Expert' is often a dirty word, for many experts, sadly, are so jealous of their status that they have closed their minds to the possibility of looking at things from a different viewpoint. But occasionally the word can be used in its proper sense of 'someone with considerable experience in a particular field'. When you are trying to decide what books to read with your child, and find the choice bewildering, the best thing to do to begin with is to go to the experts – the people who love books and children, and have spent a great deal of time finding out what happens when you put the two together.

If you are working with a child of primary school age or younger, look no further than Jill Bennett's *Learning to Read with Picture Books,* for a nucleus of irresistible books around which you can build your child's library. Then, *The Read-Aloud Handbook,* by Jim Trelease, provides an excellent list of read-aloud books for reading with children of all ages. When I was hesitantly launching our Special Education department into apprenticeship learning, I went to the bookshop armed with *The Read-Aloud Handbook,* and ordered as many titles as we could afford, that sounded appealing. An even better launch pad, however, is Elaine Moss's *Picture Books for Young People 9-13* (you can trespass on to this age range from either end), which catapulted me, in no uncertain terms, into the relatively uncharted stratosphere of picture books for older children. From then on, it was like Christmas, whenever I managed to wheedle money from one source or another, and spent it all on picture books selected from this bookguide. The children's faces, and exclamations of delight, were worth it when they dashed in and beheld the new acquisitions. "Miss! We've got some new books!"

As you gain confidence and experience, you will find that you are increasingly making your own selections and discoveries. Haunt your library and consult the librarian – again you will find that she is an expert, and knows a lot about which books are popular with children of different ages. Your local bookshop probably has a children's section, and someone with a specific interest in children's books. Other parents, who are practised in the apprenticeship approach to reading, are some of the most reliable experts around, particularly if their children are in similar circumstances to your own (age, sex, literacy 'barrier'). Many of the books that now occupy pride of place in my Special Education room were first recommended to me by parents. "Jonathan *loves* the Gumdrop books." If eleven year old Jonathan, for whom written words continually rearranged themselves in muddles, loved the Gumdrop books, then it was likely my other strugglers would love them too – and so, indeed, they do.

Edward's history makes it clear that dyslexic adolescents for whom reading has always been difficult need massive amounts of input if they are to tackle books confidently and enjoyably. The snag is that adolescence is often the time of moods and rebellion, transitory periods of not wanting to have anything to do with your parents, and the growing desire to feel independent and self reliant. Modern technology is beckoning its seductive finger. You may well be able to establish reading sessions with such a son or daughter (and you should keep trying), but you will have to pick your moment. In the meantime, provide him or her with a good quality tape recorder, and a plentiful supply of reading material on tape. Tapes that match books word for word provide the same sort of reading experience that you do in reading sessions, so your child can hardly do too much of this sort of listening and following. (Negotiate a schedule whereby she agrees to spend specific times on this, if it seems a good idea.) Do not sneer at the *Story Teller* magazines with word for word cassettes, available from newsagents; but many delectable books have now been taped 'cover to cover'. Your bookshop can advise you about what is on offer. Puffin issue a varied collection, while Tempo Tapes, from Collins, have recorded several of the Roald Dahls (see below). Roald Dahl must have done more than any other single author to entice previously resistant tearaways into the delights of reading. By the time they've followed *Fantastic Mr Fox, The Twits, George's Marvellous Medicine,* and *Revolting Rhymes,* cocooned in a pair of headphones and chortling to themselves, they are virtually hooked. Reading has become a habit, and no longer holds any terrors: almost without noticing they will begin to tackle further books without the tapes ... For now they are convinced that books belong to them.

Cover to Cover Cassettes provide a mail order service, ranging from children's titles to adult classics. The books are brought to life by many of our most outstanding actors and actresses (Jane Lapotaire, Anna Massey, Patricia Routledge, Ian Holm, Timothy West, among others). Word for word tapes for lengthier books are naturally expensive, but an investment in one or two may be sufficient to give your child the feeling of independent reading, and an introduction to great authors. Write for a catalogue to: Cover to Cover Cassettes Ltd, Ramsbury House, Hungerford, Berkshire RG17 0LY.

Struggling readers find it much easier to respond to written language of a reasonable size, in well spaced lines. Wodges of tightly packed print are too much for them. Many books for young people, which are perfectly accessible in terms of content, are off putting simply because the print is too small. When the strugglers have become practised readers, they will be able to take small print in their stride, because they will be more familiar with the way words are 'supposed to look'. They will see what they expect to see. In the meantime, you have to get them over the hump.

For example, when you are helping your child to branch out from the gorgeous picture books I've described, and include ordinary paperbacks in her experience, go first for the ones in slightly larger print. Roald Dahl's *The Twits, George's Marvellous Medicine, Charlie and the Chocolate Factory* are good for starters, shrinking a bit to *Fantastic Mr Fox, The BFG* and *Danny the Champion of the World* (Puffin). Jill Murphy's 'Worst Witch' books (*The Worst Witch, The Worst Witch Strikes Again* and *A Bad Spell for the Worst Witch,* Puffin) appeal especially to girls, and again the print is a healthy size. One of my first year girls loved them so, she wrote to Jill Murphy demanding more books about the scatter brained student witches. She had a delightful reply written in white ink on black paper, in an envelope embossed with sinister looking bats. Sarah was quite speechless with joy – but so far, no more books!

Don't overlook poetry books during this transition stage – or indeed ever. The print size in many poetry books is helpful, and the lay out, rhythm and rhyme are likewise encouraging. (Quite apart from the fact that poetry is every child's birthright.) Go for the lushly illustrated ones: *The Oxford Book of Children's Verse* (OUP), Roald Dahl's *Revolting Rhymes* and *Dirty Beasts* (Puffin), and move on to Shel Silverstein's *Where the Sidewalk Ends* (Jonathan Cape) and Kit Wright's *Hot Dog* and *Rabbiting On* (Kestrel Books).

Another way of giving your child the confidence that she really can cope with smaller print, is to 'do an Edward' and borrow from a library a large illustrated version of a book like *The Hobbit* (Unwin), which you read together – and then buy the paperback for her to keep and re-read independently. *The Hobbit's* artist, Michael Hague, has illustrated *The Wizard of Oz* (Methuen) just as powerfully, and it opened up the whole world of books for first year Nikki. Emboldened by a Christmas showing of the Judy Garland film, she asked a volunteer to read the book to her, but her initial reaction was indignant. "It's not right, it's all different from the film, I don't remember any of this – and look, they're wearing green spectacles!" I explained mildly that it wasn't possible to make a film of a whole book, and parts of it had to be left out, but that as a matter of fact the book had been written first. This was a new idea for Nikki, and gradually the book claimed her on its own terms.

She was scornful, however, when I asked her how she was getting on with the paperback. "I can't read that, Miss, it's much too difficult." "Don't be daft, Nikki, you can read the big one in school, can't you? Well, you can read the little one – the words are exactly the same." "*Are* they Miss?" and she spent the next ten minutes comparing both versions, at last reaching the joyous conclusion that I was quite right: "I never realized that before!" She began to report reading whole chapters at home, and after a while commented sorrowfully, "I wish they'd put the green spectacles in the film, I think they're brilliant." (I had a little grin to myself.) She tackled further books with confidence, but *The Wizard of Oz* was always her first love: when she and her mother came in for an evening session, it was lifted reverently from its place on the shelf, and spread out for the two of them to wonder at. "Look at this picture, Mum – and look at this one, and this one. Isn't it gorgeous?"

I reflected on everything it had taught her. That books and films could be about the same thing, but had their own separate purposes, neither one being 'better' or 'worse' than the other. She had learned to approach both critically: 'How would *I* make this film, or write this book?' and to revise her thinking as she went along. She had discovered that books were available in different versions, and that she could read ordinary paperbacks with ease and pleasure. More than all, she had learned that some books at least were magic, passports to an enchanted country where she could wander about at will.

It goes without saying that none of this would have happened if I'd simply put Nikki on the next book in a reading scheme! Nor could I have prescribed it in a syllabus written for her in advance, for I had had no idea of the learning that would emerge. In fact I'd had very little to do with the proceedings, and hadn't even shared in the reading. What had happened had taken place between Nikki and the makers of that beautiful book: the author, the artist, the publisher and the printer. Nikki's reading partner and I had been witnesses merely, but just being there had been worth it.

So always keep in mind that you want to help your child by making 'difficult' reading easy, not by making 'easy' reading difficult. As another way in to small print, you might consider investing in a good quality magnifying glass, from an optician, for use with the more adult paperbacks. Or, buy some transparent coloured plastic folders, and place a black and white sheet of printed paper in each, and see if you child finds any of them easier to read. If so, it would be worth pursuing the idea of getting plain tinted lenses for her to use when reading, and the same coloured paper for her to write on.

The barriers to reading are only apparent, not real. Another of my students, a dyslexic girl of thirteen, explained to me how she tackled books she wanted to read, but found daunting. Instinctively she used a metaphor that many of us are finding illuminating. "It's as if there's a guard at the gate, and he's trying to stop me from getting in. But he's quite harmless really, and what I do, I just walk up to him, and give him my 'no nonsense' stare, and then I can get past him, into the book."

"It's as if theres a guard at the gate, and he's trying to stop me from getting in."

IX

A note to teachers

The apprenticeship approach is steadily gaining ground in primary education, and Liz Waterland's book, *Read with Me, An Apprenticeship Approach to Reading,* provides a triumphant account of how easily an entire school can be organized along apprenticeship lines.

Secondary education is a different matter. If, as a teacher in secondary education, you are unfamiliar with the apprenticeship approach, but would like to try it, and to share the approach with parents, it is a good idea to set up a 'pilot project' with one child. (Say two sessions a week during the lunch hour, or right after school.) Don't tackle just reading, but include tallying words (Book Two) and writing (Book Three). Document what you do as thoroughly as possible. This will enable you to convince the administration of the effectiveness of apprenticeship, and also give you confidence in your sessions with parents. You will know that it works because you have done it yourself.

It is then comparatively easy to map out ways of teaching 'one-to-one' even in the context of a group. (I have groups of up to eight children.) While you are working one-to-one with a child, the rest are getting on individually or in pairs, using the computer, listening to tapes, exploring books, drawing, typing, doing *Headwork* (O.U.P.) or *Catchwords* (Harcourt Brace Jovanovich) exercises, or working with another adult. Every half hour you all move round and do something else.

The best way of involving mainstream teachers is to point out that they have probably taught their own children in this very same fashion, without realizing it. I find that my colleagues get hooked on apprenticeship when I start discussing ways of tackling their own children's spelling difficulties. (It's surprising how many teachers' children have a struggle with spelling – their parents usually think it's just 'one of those things' and you can't do anything about it!) When they have experienced the extension of their natural apprenticeship way of teaching their own children, to reading and/or spelling, they begin to find methods of using the approach even in a class of thirty. A good one is to encourage the children to help each other; and we are finding that it is the children who are only slightly ahead of the 'strugglers' who are the most effective teachers, rather than the most able. This gives the 'tutors' the appreciation and recognition they have often lacked in the past: you can praise both 'tutor' and 'tutee' for the work they do together, so everybody is happy.

A book list for you

The mass of research material about the teaching of reading would stretch from here to the moon and back again. Fortunately you can ignore most of it as it is beside the point. What a good deal of research does not recognise is that the definition of 'reading' is crucial. Many theorists simply assume that learning to read = learning to say written words aloud, and following this signpost they go galloping off in the wrong direction entirely. Also, much research concentrates on finding out why children 'fail', which again misdirects the attention.

Theory is never 'mere' theory. It is theory that defines the terms and asks the questions, and if our definitions are hopelessly inaccurate, and we are asking the wrong questions, then the resulting practice is bound to be ineffective at best, or harmful at worst.

When you decide to pursue the history of the idea that real reading is a matter of seeing meanings in written words, you have embarked on a fascinating journey. Here are some mileposts. (I've divided the books into three rough categories: a) Theory and research. b) The practitioners. c) Firsthand experiences – although some titles straddle more than one section.)

a) *Theory and research*

E.B. Huey, *The Psychology and Pedagogy of Reading* (1908; Massachusetts Institute of Technology Press, 1972)

> This is an absorbing book which demonstrates vividly that 'there is nothing new under the sun'. As long ago as 1908, Huey, an outstanding psychologist of the time, had reasoned his way to the insight that reading was primarily a matter of 'getting meaning from print'. He concluded further that the best teachers of reading were parents, and that 'the secret of it all lies in parents' reading aloud to and with the child'!! (p.332).

His book recounts the history of the development of written language, and surveys the many reading methods which had been and were being used. It is out of print at the moment but can be obtained from libraries.

Glenn Doman, *Teach Your Baby to Read* (1963; Cape, 1965)

This is the great 'invisible' book. As far as the academic establishment is concerned, it doesn't exist. There are several reasons for this. One is that Dr Doman is not a qualified educationist (whatever that might mean); nor is he a medical doctor. He works intensively with the parents of brain damaged children, with startling results. The vast majority of these brain damaged children learn to read fluently, much earlier than 'normal' children. In this book, which Glenn Doman wrote so that normal children could enjoy the same advantages(!) he explains why reading comes so easily to the handicapped youngsters. Reading, he points out, is like hearing. If you expose a baby to meaningful written language, in exactly the same way that she is exposed to meaningful speech, she will learn to understand it just as readily.

In other words, his unforgiveable crime is to maintain that learning to read, far from being difficult and complex, is an embarrassingly simple process, which a child of any age can easily accomplish. Worse, he goes on to say that the best people to teach reading are parents (because they are very good at teaching babies to hear). Naturally, the academic world looks straight past him; or, when forced to take some notice, it declares that his methods are unacceptable. To some extent, the academics have a point. Dr Doman's early reading vocabularies are appropriate, as the title of his book implies, for *babies*; but many mothers get bogged down with his word cards, and fail to see how to make the transition to books. He has identified the reading process, however, with exquisite precision. All that is needed is to appreciate that the best way of exposing any child to 'meaningful written language' is to read real books to her and with her.

Frank Smith, *Reading* (Cambridge University Presss, 1978)

Frank Smith is a noted academic; and so more respectable than Doman, which means that he gets an audience in schools of education and among research students as well as practising teachers. Thank heaven for that. Parents, as he makes clear in his preface, are an afterthought, but fortunately he writes so sensibly and lucidly that his book is just as relevant in the real world as in the ivory tower. He isn't quite able to make Doman's bold analogy, that reading = hearing, but defines reading as a process of 'bringing meaning to print', which boils down to the same thing. Another of his phrases which should ring in our ears for aeons yet is that 'teachers should make learning to read easy, rather than make it difficult'.

I part company with him when he rejects the teaching of phonics (because all the 'irregularities' result in an unpredictable system). He is quite right that learning phonics has nothing whatever to do with real reading; but in Book Two of this series I shall try to show that it is an entirely separate process, valid in its own right, essential for accurate spelling, and easily mastered; but many children need specific help if they are to operate the system of 'phonetic matching' properly.

I also think that he misses the point about dyslexia. His view is one where I stuck for many years. If children can see tables, chairs, other people, roads, cars, trees and houses perfectly clearly thankyou, how on earth can we suppose that they see written words – backwards? Distinguishing between seeing written words and visualizing their mental images helps us to understand where the trouble lies: that dyslexia is a visual*izing* problem, not a visual one; and that it is in this sense children can be said to be 'word blind'. What they need from their teachers, however, is exactly what all other children need – they simply need more of it, if they are to get through their 'visualizing barrier'.

71

Margaret Clark, *Young Fluent Readers* (Heinemann, 1976)

As I've said, most research into the teaching of reading concentrates on pinpointing the causes of 'failure'. In 1969, Margaret Clark and her fellow researchers decided instead to try to pinpoint the causes of *success*. Thirty two children who were already reading fluently and with understanding when they started school at five years old formed the basis for the study. How could it be that children who had not attended school, and had never ploughed their way through all the stages of a graded reading scheme, were nevertheless reading silently and with total absorption, often at the 11 – 12 year old level, all manner of books including adult fiction?!

The common factors she discovered: there was almost always at least one adult who had plenty of time to read to the child, listen to her and answer her questions. This adult rarely set out to teach the child to read, and was usually the one who did the reading at first – the child was seldom if every required to read to the adult. Very few of the children attended nursery school. The mother often preferred to have her children with her, took a keen interest in what they were doing, and actively enjoyed spending time at home with them. The children who were studied, far from being misfits at school, adjusted well and happily to their new environment.

Jennie Ingham, *Books and Reading Development* (Heinemann, 1981)

The research which is the subject of this book has enormous importance, and yet it makes you want to cry: it should never have needed to be done. Once we re-define learning to read as 'learning to become involved with books' it seems obvious that children who are given more books to read will become involved with more books! And yet the results of the 'Bradford Book Flood' experiment were by no means predictable. The 'book flood' was exactly that: starting in 1977, certain Bradford middle schools were 'flooded' with books, in an attempt to discover whether this would make a real difference to the reading experience of the children involved. Insistently, however, the deepest roots of real reading nourishment were revealed. It was the children whose *homes* were naturally 'flooded' with books who were the most avid readers. We have assumed for so long that the schools are the repositories of 'book learning'; and that if parents do any teaching at home, they should try to do it 'like teachers'. But what seems to be emerging now, at every point, is that if teachers want their pupils to love reading and writing, they are going to have to start teaching *like parents*. One headmaster in the experiment indicated as much, almost unconsciously. 'What the head would *like* to be able to do,' declares the author, 'is to provide children in school with the variety of books available to children in fairly well off, literary homes; similarly, what he would *like* to do would be to give children the opportunity for one-to-one conversation with adults, such as a few fortunate children have with their parents . . .'

Susanne Langer, *Philosophy in a New Key: A Study in the Symbolism of Reason Rite and Art* (Harvard University Press, 1942)

Many theorists compare print with speech, but most go on from there to compare learning to read with learning to talk. The child's first involvement with spoken language is assumed to be her first *utterance*. Only Doman, that I know of, has made the tremendously significant metaphorical leap of comparing reading with *hearing*. Of course he is right; and this means that if we want to shed light on the teaching of reading by pursuing the comparison between written and spoken language, we must examine first what happens when children learn to hear. How do spoken words convey meanings? The reason that psychology hasn't attempted this task is that it is not the province of the psychologist: it is the province of the philosopher. Susanne Langer's brilliant work has charted the entire territory, by showing that what makes human beings unique is their ability to employ and understand symbols – she defines a symbol, with crystal elegance, as 'any device whereby we are enabled to make an abstraction'. This definition immediately delineates the real and enormous difference between words and letters. Words (whether spoken or written) are symbols, because they represent abstractions. Letters, like isolated sounds, are merely signs; and what letters and sounds signify is each other. The two basic mental processes involved in our response to language fall into place, therefore, in the flash of a definition. Her work is illuminating throughout, but now, sadly, out of print. I can only hope that some enlightened publisher will reprint it.

Seton Pollock, *The Basic Colour Factor Guide* (Heinemann, 1965)

Mathematics isn't primarily 'about' numbers. Numbers are just some of the symbols mathematicians can use to express various mathematical ideas. The ideas themselves lie at the heart of all our thinking, and find their first expression, not in numbers, but in language (e.g. tallying; operations on sets; adding, subtracting, multiplying and dividing; identifying the highest common factors and the lowest common multiples; appreciating ratio). In this book, which is the most fascinating work on teaching mathematics I have read, Seton Pollock explores these parallels, among many others.

S.T. Orton, *Reading, Writing and Speech Problems in Children* (Chapman and Hall, 1937)

The debate over whether we should use the term 'dyslexia' or 'specific learning difficulty' has a tortuous history. At one time I thought it didn't matter what you called it so long as you did something about it. I now feel that the expression 'learning difficulty' (whether specific or otherwise) is very misleading, implying as it does that there is something wrong with the *way* the child learns. It seems to me that there is nothing wrong with the way any child learns; but a high proportion of children have difficulty in learning *by means of reading*, and in demonstrating their understanding *by means of writing.* They have a 'literacy problem' – their ability to read and write is malfunctioning, which is precisely the meaning of 'dys-lexia'.

Orton's work attributes this malfunction to a confusion of the images perceived in both hemispheres of the brain. He suggests yet another term for the condition, 'strephosymbolia', or 'twisted symbols', which is even more accurate than the term 'dyslexia' – it makes clear that the symbols stay twisted even when the resulting literacy problems have been solved. (I.e. just because a dyslexic child learns to read and write fluently does not mean that her dyslexia has vanished!) But since the word 'dyslexia' is in such common use, we might as well stick with that – and try deriving an adjective from 'strephosymbolia'.

b) *Now, the practitioners:*

Liz Waterland, *Read with Me, an Apprenticeship Approach to Reading* (Thimble Press, 1985)

If parents are the best teachers of reading, the prospects look dim for all the children who have to learn to read in school. It is, of course, impossible for school teachers to teach 'like parents'.

No one has explained to Liz Waterland that this is impossible. She has therefore been instrumental in re-organizing several schools so that all the teachers do indeed teach 'like parents'.

No one has explained to Liz Waterland that whatever 'cultured' parents might be able to achieve, 'ordinary' parents cannot possibly help their own children to read and write. So virtually all the parents of her pupils read and explore books with their own children. The triumph of her breakthrough can best be summed up in the words of one parent who came to a parents' evening just to say, 'Our Elaine's done lovely at this school. She'll be anything now. Mind, if I'd had them books, I could've been anything too.'

Read with Me describes exactly how the impossible has been achieved: how ordinary teachers have worked alongside ordinary parents so that the children's *homes* are 'flooded with books'. And if we can flood the homes of our primary school children with books, who knows what we can achieve next?

Jim Trelease, *The Read-Aloud Handbook* (Penguin, 1982)

Jim Trelease is an American journalist. Almost by chance he found himself visiting schools and reading aloud to the children there. In this way he was able to share his own passion for books with many youngsters. *The Read-Aloud Handbook* recounts some of his experiences, and includes a first rate list of books, compiled for English readers by Jill Bennett, which are suitable for reading aloud to children of all ages.

Jill Bennett, *Learning to Read with Picture Books* (Thimble Press, 1979)

Since 'easy reading material' in fact makes reading difficult, because the learner is never exposed to a varied and interesting written vocabulary, it follows that 'graded readers' are the biggest barriers of all, on the road to fluent literacy. In *Learning to Read with Picture Books*, Jill Bennett shows how reading can be introduced in schools without ever having recourse to those travesties of real reading, 'reading schemes'. Her book lists are simply mouth watering feasts – but as she is at pains to make clear, only 'tasters', by no means exclusive. So draw up a chair and tuck in!

Elaine Moss, *Picture Books for Young People 9 – 13* (Thimble Press, 1981)

And if you thought picture books were only for infants, think again.

Margaret Meek, *Learning to Read* (Bodley Head, 1982)

The language which truly nourishes all our children must be real language. Margaret Meek points out that book language is real language. It's just a different kind of real language from speech. And it does not inhabit reading schemes. This book adds its clarion call to the swelling refrain: 'a reading scheme is a series of books written by no one for everyone' (*Learning to Read* p.100). Mrs Meek, herself an expert in the best sense, offers a wealth of practical advice to parents who want their children to fall in love with real books.

Tony Martin, *The Strugglers* (Open University Press, 1989)

Once we appreciate that there are two entirely separate ways of operating on print (seeing the meaning, and seeing the sounds), we can become more aware of just how to support the 'strugglers'.

What has misled us for so long is the fact that if you help most children to operate either process, they will end up teaching themselves to operate the other one! If you teach a child to 'sound out' written words, she will gradually become able to 'see the meanings', as a result. Or, if you help her to 'see the meanings' first, she will automatically murmur the words aloud, so establishing a multitude of associations between shapes and sounds. Most of my strugglers, in fact, do learn to read aloud by means of abundant reading input, and a modest amount of 'reading back'. (See Section VII.)

The snag is that there are a very few children - like Edward - who don't. Because it is so much easier for Edward to read silently, without reference to inner speech, he doesn't automatically form the associations between shapes and sounds which for most children are a byproduct of real reading. (See Book Three, Section V.)

It's not that associating shapes and sounds is a difficult process. On the contrary, it is very simple and basic, and Edward can do it when he has to. But he *doesn't* do it when he's reading - whch is why reading aloud is so much more of a 'struggle' for him. He has consciously to 'change gear', and start trying to decide on the spoken words which match the written words he sees.

Unfortunately, the ability to read aloud is a vital foundation for accuracy in writing and spelling. So we must make sure that we provide the Edwards of this world with the extensive experience of reading aloud which they are not providing for themselves.

Tony Martin's book blazes the way. The solution he has discovered is a variation of 'paired reading'. It avoids all the pitfalls of conventional paired reading, and capitalizes on its strengths.

I'm unhappy about conventional paired reading because it puts too much emphasis on the process of reading aloud at the outset, assuming that this is what learning to read is all about. (See p. 41.) It's fine for children who have already learned to enjoy books, who have had considerable exposure to meaningful print, and who do not have severe visualizing problems. For them, paired reading does indeed provide enjoyable supported practice in the art of reading aloud.

However, for many strugglers, it starts too far ahead of where they are. What they need initially is the experience of wallowing in all sorts of delicious books, and massive exposure to meaningful print, without any pressure to 'perform'. Once they are established as real readers, though, 'paired reading' can come into its own.

Tony Martin, like Liz Waterland, puts real books first, second and last. So he has developed what is essentially the apprenticeship appproach to reading – very much my own abundant reading *to* a child, followed by the child reading back a small amount. But in the middle – this is the crafty bit that I hadn't thought of – he sandwiches two 'paired reading' sections: tutor and child reading aloud together, with first the tutor leading, then the child. (See *The Strugglers*, p. 52.) Simple, but brilliant. I have tried it with Edward, and it's very effective.

It isn't the whole answer. Ultimately, Edward has to develop the tallying way of looking at print, for every word he sees, so as to be sure of reading it aloud accurately. (See Book Two, and Book Three, Section V.) But Tony Martin's approach lays the groundwork for this, and makes it much easier for the Edwards to associate print with speech just like everybody else, 'without having to think about it', as a byproduct of real reading.

I think that, having been schooled by Frank Smith, he too misses the point about dyslexia, but this in no way affects the quality of his work. Much of it is devoted to accounts of real conversations he had with his strugglers: "What did it feel like, why do you think you couldn't read, is that when you gave up, what did you think was the point . . .?" followed by faithful transcriptions of what the youngsters actually thought about the whole business. And there is a brilliant final chapter which describes exciting and sensitive ways of choosing, introducing and discussing books and authors. Not to be missed!

c) *Last but not least, the learners themselves:*

Dorothy Butler, *Cushla and Her Books* (Hodder, 1979)

> Cushla, in infancy, was diagnosed as severely mentally and physically retarded. Doctors recommended that she be institutionalized. However, her parents put her on a 'dose' of fourteen read-aloud books a day. By the age of five she was reading independently, and the psychologists found her to be 'well above average in intelligence and a socially well adjusted child'.

Susan Hampshire, *Susan's Story* (Sidgwick and Jackson, 1981)

> A first hand account, by a well known actress, of what it feels like to be dyslexic. No one can read this book and still suppose that the dyslexia has disappeared when the sufferer is able to read!

Helen Keller, *The Story of My Life* (Doubleday and Company, 1902)

The only means of understanding possessed by Helen Keller were her fingers.When she was one and a half, an acute fever left her blind and deaf. When she was nearly seven, Anne Sullivan entered her life. Miss Sullivan was untrained, but had nearly lost her own eyesight: she had learned the manual alphabet, and to read braille. So taking in her own the fingers of this small, wilful, imprisoned child, she forged a bridge between Helen and the world. *The Story of my Life* shows how few were the nooks and crannies of this world which Helen Keller was unable to explore, or to portray in her own rich and flowing language.

THE NATURAL WAY TO LEARN

THE APPRENTICESHIP APPROACH TO LITERACY

BOOK TWO

Seeing Sounds, Hearing Shapes

SAYING WRITTEN WORDS ALOUD

Felicity Craig

CONTENTS BOOK 2

Illustrated by
Tim Sherwin, Adam Bowhay, Edward Dart,
Jonathan Sullivan, Lee Barlow

'I should see the garden far better,' said Alice to herself, 'if I could get to the top of that hill: and here's a path that leads straight to it – at least, no, it doesn't do that –' (after going a few yards along the path, and turning several sharp corners), 'but I suppose it will at last. But how curiously it twists! It's more like a corkscrew than a path! Well, *this* turn goes to the hill, I suppose – no, it doesn't! This goes straight back to the house! Well then, I'll try it the other way.'

Lewis Carroll
Through the Looking Glass

I

What is happening when your child learns to read aloud?

Immediately we are faced with another paradox: what is going on is not at all what we think.

For a start, 'saying written words aloud' has virtually nothing to do with real reading. Deaf children have been taught to understand print very readily without reference to speech.[1] So, in fact, have hearing children.[2] And all fluent readers learn to understand many new words, not by hearing them, but by reading them.

If reading aloud is not the same as real reading, then what *is* it the same as? Once again, we have overlooked the answer to this one because it is so staggeringly simple. We say written words aloud not in order to understand them. We say written words aloud – in order to *say* them. No less, and no more. As we do so, the meanings of spoken words can be transferred to written words; and the meanings of written words can be transferred to spoken words.

Just as the process underlying our understanding of words is a profoundly mathematical one, so too is the process whereby we match one form of language with another. Mathematicians call it 'tallying', and all children can tally from the moment when they first sit up and take notice (if not before). It is a matter of linking two separate items as a pair.

So, a hungry baby stops crying when his mother picks him up, or when he sees the bottle, because this means he is going to be fed. His dad says, "Where's Mummy?" and he cranes his head round to look for her. His older sister buttons him into his coat and puts his woolly hat on, and he makes for the front door, confidently expecting to be taken outside.

The ability to associate two things in this way is the basis, not only of human intelligence, but of all animal intelligence. The classic example is Pavlov's dog, producing saliva when a bell rang, even though it couldn't see its dinner plate. It had learned to associate the sound of the bell with food, and so responded to the bell as if to the sight of its meal. A useful way of describing the procedure is to say that we are tallying 'signs' with 'objects'. The 'object' is what interests us, and the 'sign' indicates the object in some way.[3] The baby's bottle indicates that he is about to be fed; the pattern of sounds 'Mummy' indicates his mother; coats and hats indicate the Great Outdoors, and the bell indicates food. An interesting feature of the sign – object relationship is that it is entirely reversible. Lightning is a sign that there is going to be thunder; thunder is a sign that there has been lightning. It just depends which one happens to interest us more at the moment. That is then the 'object', and the other one functions as the 'sign'.

The two forms of language, written and spoken, are associated in this very same way. They are equivalent. Neither form depends on its reference to the other in order to convey meaning. But they tally, one to one. The written word 'chair' is tallied with the matching pattern of sounds. If we learn the meaning of the spoken word first, then we can respond to the written word 'chair' as a 'sign' indicating the meaningful spoken work. The more we do this, the more closely the meaning becomes identified with the written word itself, until, when we see it, we can think of the meaning directly, without having to go by way of the spoken version.

But this process also works the other way round. If we learn the meaning of the *written* word first (as my daughter learned the meaning of 'moustache', by reading it), we can use that as the 'object', learning to understand the spoken word by visualizing the matching written word.

Search your own experience of language, and you can probably find instances where this has happened. For example, when like most children of my generation I was devouring all the Enid Blyton books I could get hold of, I used to pronounce the written word 'decent' 'dick-*ent*' to myself. I knew perfectly well what it meant. It was a rather self righteous word. All the little prigs in Enid Blyton's books went around being jolly 'dickent' to each other. One day it dawned on me that the word shouldn't be pronounced 'dickent' at all, but 'dee-sent'! Fancy that! I already knew the meaning of 'decent' as a separate (and much nicer) spoken word. If my father said of someone, "Ron is a decent bloke," that meant Ron was definitely all right. But now this spoken word assumed all the additional overtones of 'dickent' – and became somewhat tarnished as a result. In this case the written word was transferring its own meaning to the spoken word.

The more time we spend reading, the more this happens, without our being particularly aware of it. But linking print with speech is always a two way process. As soon as we have learned to associate a written word with a spoken word, that spoken word will inevitably signify the written word.

Footnotes

1. See Helen Thompson, *An Experimental Study of the Beginning Reading of Deaf Mutes*. New York: Columbia University Press, 1927.

2. See James E. McDade, 'A Hypothesis for Non Oral Reading', *The Journal of Educational Research*. Washington D.C.: Heldref Publications, 1937.

3. See Susanne Langer, *Philosophy in a New Key*, p.58.

II

The 'meaning' bridge between print and speech

There are two paths to associating written words with spoken words. One is via the common meaning. If a child takes note of a written word in a pictorial context, or a physical context, the meaning is so immediate that the link between the meaning and the written word probably happens first. Suppose he sees a picture of an umbrella, with the written word next to it, in large clear letters. The idea of 'umbrellaness', of mushroom shaped pieces of nylon sliding up and down on a stick which you carry when it's raining, begins straightaway to graft itself onto the pattern of shapes in front of him. But he already has a pattern of sounds for that idea. So when he looks at the written word, he thinks of the meaning, and the spoken word comes too. This also happens when he uses the rest of the sentence as a context to find out the meaning of an unfamiliar written word. If he reads 'Mary is carrying an umbrella because it is raining,' and works out the meaning of the word 'umbrella' from his understanding of the other words in the sentence, then once again, the meaning of the word comes first, bringing the spoken word along with it.

Because patterns of shapes can convey meanings just as directly as patterns of sounds, some written languages concentrate on the 'meaning' link, and don't bother particularly about the link with speech. These are the ideographic languages, such as written Chinese, where written words begin as direct pictures of an idea. As time goes on, they become increasingly stylized, so that the meaning isn't immediately obvious just from looking at the word, but they still operate without any clear connection with the spoken forms. This can be an advantage. Chinese who speak many different dialects are still able to understand their written language, because it conveys meanings rather than spoken words. They just fit their own spoken words to the written ones.

Theorists often shake their heads wisely and say that it is very difficult to learn to read an ideographic language, because there are so many different words to remember; but of course it isn't. It is no more difficult learning to read a multitude of different words than it is to learn to hear them. Language is made of all sorts of different words, and the human mind is perfectly designed to take note of them and distinguish between them. If it can do it with patterns of sounds, it can do it with patterns of shapes – and in fact it does learn each and every written word as a particular and individual pattern, whether the language is ideographic or phonetic. (Think – how do you *know* the way 'bed' looks, and the way 'said' looks? Although the endings of both words match the same sound, you have no difficulty in visualizing the difference in spelling.)

In April 1971, the *Observer* printed a report about tests which had been carried out in a Philadelphia school. The children concerned had been trying to learn to read in English, with little success, for one and a half years. They had been taught by a phonic 'method', but still couldn't even read words like 'pip' and 'lag'. So the researchers decided to teach them to read Chinese instead. (Well, why not?)

Here are some of the first Chinese characters which the Philadelphia children learned to read, together with their meanings:

(The children learned to say these words in English, not spoken Chinese.)

After only two and a half to five and a half hours, these children, who had been wrestling aridly with pips and lags and rods and tubs for months on end, found that they could read up to thirty Chinese characters each. And they enjoyed it.

The implications of this exercise were sadly missed by the researchers, who surveyed the evidence and plumped for a 'reading' method based on the *syllable*. (?!) The point that seems obvious to me is that it is quite easy to work out the sounds for words like 'pip', 'lag', 'rod' and 'tub'. *But it isn't easy to read them.* On the other hand, the Chinese characters for 'mother', 'big' and 'knife' are large and clear, and the meanings of those words carry an emotional charge which is quite lacking from 'pip', 'lag' and so forth. Naturally the Philadelphia children found it very easy to learn to read the Chinese words. (They would have coped with the equivalent English words just as readily, if it had occurred to the researchers to present them, in the same way.)

My elder daughter Helen, who fell in love with books at the age of three, and has read voraciously ever since, decided out of the blue that what she most wanted to study at university was Chinese. She has had no trouble in learning to read the language, and I often think that this is partly because, when she learned to read English words, it was the meaning that came first.

III

The 'phonetic' bridge

It may be just as easy to read an ideographic language as a phonetic one. It is a different matter entirely when it comes to writing it.

Spoken words are very simple to produce. The human voice has to function within its limitations, the main one being that it has only a comparatively small number of different sounds to play around with. (In English we use about forty.) So it is out of the question to invent a new sound for every new word.

However, we haven't let that stop us. We have used each separate sound as just part of a word, and we have strung the separate sounds together to form patterns. It is the patterns that are unique.

Because forty different items can be rearranged in a virtually infinite number of permutations (mathematics again!), with these forty sounds we can generate a virtually infinite number of different spoken words. (Well, thousands and thousands anyway, which is more than enough for any mere mortal.) So the process of inventing new words knows no bounds, and carries on apace.

It is at this point that an ideographic written language runs into trouble. Evey time you think of a new word, you have to think of a new shape for that word, and by the time you get into the thousands, it isn't easy. It is surprising how ingeniously ideographic languages cope with this problem, but it still means that the task of the scribe (though not of the reader) is an uphill struggle. You can't use keyboards, or movable print; compared with speech, the written language staggers on laboriously, miles behind.

Thousands of years ago, one of the greatest inventors who ever lived had an inspiration that was sheer genius. (He probably lived somewhere in the Middle East.) It struck him that the solution to the problem was to set out in the opposite direction. Instead of racking your brains to think of yet more

15

and more shapes whose meanings were obvious, all you had to do was to devise a small number of shapes that were entirely meaning*less*. And this was the point. With a set of meaningless shapes, you could produce an infinite number of written words, *in just the same way that you produced spoken words*. The individual sounds in spoken words were without meaning: it was only when you put them together that the meaning emerged, as if by magic.[4] So if you invented shapes to match the separate sounds – you could then proceed to generate written words in the same economical way as speech.[5]

The rest, as they say, is history. Quite literally, because it was the invention of the alphabet which enabled history to be recorded, to any great extent.

Unfortunately we haven't fully appreciated the true brilliance of our invention. We persist in thinking that a phonetic script is a good idea because it enables us to work out the sounds for written words, and learn to read that way. But the detailed match with speech is a mere spin-off from the real achievement of generating written words like spoken words.

However, the match is there; and since it is there, we might as well make use of it. In a phonetic language, written words are composed of shapes that correspond to individual sounds in spoken words. This means that as well as linking written words with spoken words via their meanings, we can match each shape in a word with a sound, and therefore associate the whole written word with an equivalent spoken word – by way of the 'phonetic' bridge.

Interestingly enough, this is just as true of 'irregular' words as it is of regular ones. Even for an 'irregular' word, the match between shapes and sounds still operates, and the left-to-right order of the letters still follows the sequence of sounds in the spoken word. When a child looks at the written word 'cough' and says 'coff', he sees the 'cu' sound matching the letter 'c', and the 'off' bit goes with 'ough'.

Footnotes

4. See Susane Langer, *Philosophy in a New Key*, p.75
5. See Frank Smith, *Reading*, pp. 60-61.

Why bother with phonics?

First let's examine in more detail how a child works the 'phonetic bridge'.

As I indicated in Section I, it is a tallying procedure. The child learns to tally individual shapes with individual sounds, which means that he can then tally whole written words with whole spoken words.

He can tally irregular words just as easily as regular ones: he uses the same mathematical approach. If we look at the way he tackles a horror like 'Worcestershire', we can probably appreciate more clearly what it is that he is about.

In order to tally 'Worcestershire' accurately with the matching spoken word, the child needs three things. The written word, the spoken word – *and the knowledge that they go with each other*. Then, he can get to work.

He begins by fitting the words together at the points that obviously correspond. The letter 'W' must go with the 'wu' sound. Things after that seem to be fairly haywire, but straighten themselves out again when he gets to 'ster'. On to the letters 'shire', which have to go with the 'shu' sound at the end of the spoken word; so now, back to the bit left over. The letters 'orce' must tally with the sound 'o͝o', unlikely as that may seem, because there's nothing else for them to go with, and anyway they are in the right place in the word. Done! From then on, when the child looks at the word 'Worcestershire', he 'sees' an 'o͝o' sound going with 'orce', and a 'shu' sound going with 'shire', until the irregularity of the word hardly bothers him. The spoken word has bedded itself down alongside the written word; and the child notes this without really thinking about it.

Granted that most of us engage in this procedure 'without really thinking about it'. Why do we go to these lengths? What does it help us to *do*?

It doesn't help us to understand the written word. The meaning is perfectly clear from the letters themselves. In fact the meaning 'the shire based around Wor-cester ('cester' for 'camp' linking with 'cester', 'caster' and 'chester' in other place names) is more clearly conveyed by the written word than by the spoken word. Nor does it help us to pronounce the spoken word accurately. We have already learned to do that by hearing the word. But learning the phonetic match for 'Worcestershire' has a great deal to do with *spelling* it correctly.

Most of us, when we write, mutter the words we are writing, under our breath. So writing usually involves the reverse phonetic process – we are translating from sounds back to letters. If we have learned to translate 'Worcestershire' in detail, going from shapes to sounds, we will have little difficulty in translating back again, from sounds to shapes. The 'wu' sound goes with 'W', the 'ŏŏ' sound is spelt 'orce' because we've already noted that, 'ster' is straightforward, and 'shu' matches with the 'shire' part at the end.

Several things emerge from this analysis. One is that what matters is for the child to be able to *appreciate* the phonetic match between a written word and a spoken word – *not that he should work out what the spoken word must be*. In order to do this, he needs both the written word and the spoken word at his disposal, to start off with. Then he can fit them together. Quite apart from the fact that we are ludicrously mistaken if we think a child has to be able to work out the sounds for a written word in order to read it – it is much easier to teach him *phonics* if we start with real words, out of real books, that he can already read and say aloud. He then progresses quite naturally to the point where he can begin with just the written word, and work out the spoken word. By reading aloud to a child, you are not only helping him to see the meanings in written words. You are also showing him which spoken words go with which written words, so that when he is ready he can carry out a more detailed match.

Something else to be noted is that we mustn't abandon the whole 'phonics' business when we get to so-called 'irregular' words. It is precisely when we need to spell 'irregular' words that our practised analytical technique begins to pay read dividends. Noting the 'irregularities' in one direction means that we can remember them just as easily on the way back.

It is quite true that familiarity with phonic translation does enable a child to exchange meanings between his reading vocabulary and his speech vocabulary, so that he can often find out the meaning of a new word by matching it with an equivalent form. To this extent, the process is an aid to reading – and, indeed, to speaking.

But it is when he is learning to spell that the child who cannot analyse words phonetically is at a serious disadvantage.

V

What does your child need to know?

Again, we must begin, like Alice, at the other end, and ask ourselves what a child needs to be able to do with his 'knowing'. Then we can retrace our footsteps and help him to acquire the knowledge that he has to have to do it.

What your child needs to be able to do is to appreciate the phonetic link between every single written word and its matching spoken word. (This is the best possible foundation for accurate spelling.) He will learn the phonetic match for each individual word as a unique and separate entity, and he can get to grips with all this quite easily, because his brain is designed for the purpose. (Among many other purposes, of course.) Think about it. You can do this with written words, and almost certainly you learned to do it as a child. Children can learn many times faster than adults.

Now we can ask the question: What does he need to know so that he can do this?

Not a lot.

a) He needs to know the sounds that most commonly correspond with the separate letters of the alphabet. The easiest way of identifying these is to think of them as 'sound names', and say each sound with a little 'turning up' flick at the end, which makes it easier to pronounce. (The turning up sound is readily dropped when the sounds are combined.) So the 'sound name' alphabet goes: ă, bu, cu, du, ě, fu, gu, hu, ĭ, ju, ku, lu, mu, nu, ŏ, pu, qu, ru, su, tu, ŭ, vu, wu, ex, yu, zu.

b) He needs to know the letter names for the five vowels ā, ē, ī, ō, ū, and the consonants c and g. (He can learn the letter names for the whole alphabet at this point if you wish, but only the letter names I've mentioned are necessary for phonetic matching.)

c) He needs to know that certain combinations of letters can be matched with single unified sounds that are not the same as the sounds matching the separate letters. These are: ai, au, aw, ay, ch, ea, ee, er, ir, ur, ar, or, ew, ng, oa, oo, ou, ow, ph, sh, th, ui.

d) He needs to know a little bit about 'alphabet magic', so he can see how the letters 'e' 'i' and 'y' change the sounds of other letters.

e) He needs to be able to analyse written words from left to right, so that he lines up sounds with letters, in the proper order.

And that's it.

VI

Learning what he needs to know

The nice thing about learning these things is that he doesn't have to tackle them in any particular sequence. Forget all the wise pronouncements you have heard about 'structured learning'. Language does indeed have a structure, but it is natural and organic. If you want to understand what a tree is all about, you can learn about the leaves first, or the roots, or the trunk, or the bark. Everything else is still there, and you can get to it when you are ready. (Of course it is a bit silly to examine leaves under a microscope unless you already know that they are part of a *tree*.) Nevertheless, as you study the way written words are linked with spoken words, there is a definite progression, just as there is in a tree, from roots up to leaves, and if you have this structure clearly in mind, you will be well equipped to explain it to your child so that it makes sense.

You begin teaching your child to link shapes with sounds as soon as you start reading aloud to him, holding the book so he can see the print. The meanings are what matter, but the sounds come with the meanings, willy nilly. The link becomes clearer still as your child learns to say written words aloud himself. Again, the emphasis is on the meaning, but the additional association with sounds is inevitable. As he reads aloud more and more, he is also bound to notice that words containing the same shapes match words containing the same sounds. 'Pig' and 'pin' have identical letters at one edge, and the matching spoken words start with the same sounds. Maybe we are onto something here.

We are indeed. It has dawned on your child that as well as tallying whole words, *he can also tally the bits.* And tallying the bits helps him to tally the same bits in other words, so that he can tally those words as well – and more bits, and more words – and really, there is more to this thing than first occurred.

By reading aloud, he can teach himself a great deal about the links between letters and sounds, but you don't have to leave it entirely to him. You might as well give him a helping hand, in this exciting undertaking of 'tallying the bits', and provide him with the sounds for all the letters of the alphabet. What you will be doing as you embark on this, is making clear to him something that is already happening, so you will use his ability to tally whole written words with whole spoken words, as a starting point.

As we've already noticed, the easiest way of learning to associate a written word with a spoken word is via the common meaning. Most alphabet books for young children do this very sensibly with the help of delicious pictures: buy the most scrumptious one you can afford. The picture of the apple provides the meaning for the written word alongside it, and this helps your child to think of the spoken word that matches the written word. But the initial 'a' is probably picked out in a bright contrasting colour, signalling that it matches just the first sound in the spoken word.

When you are reading an alphabet book with your child, encourage him to say the word while he is looking at the written form. The picture is there to remind him – you are not 'testing' him, but helping him to learn. Then cover all the letters in the written word, except for the initial one, and tell him the sound name for that letter. "Oh look – that letter by itself says 'ă' – 'ă' for 'apple'. You say it!" And so on, reading together as many pages as you wish. Almost certainly, if it is an attractive book, your child will wander through it several times on his own, playing this new game of reading the words, and then matching initial sounds to initial letters.

If you prefer, you can always make an alphabet book, together with your child. Choose a word beginning with each letter-sound in the alphabet (the short sounds for the vowels – good ones for these are apple, elephant, indian, octopus and umbrella) and then help him to draw, paint or cut out a picture to match each word. Glue the picture onto one page in a scrap book, and underneath, write the word that goes with it, in thick clear letters. (If the pages of the scrap book are too absorbent, and the lettering would smudge, write the word on a separate piece of paper, and glue that in too.)

The initial letter should be written in a bright contrasting colour. For good measure, write the word again, this time beginning with a capital letter. On the page opposite, write just the letter by itself with its capital form, so your child can practise matching sounds to isolated letters.

Making an alphabet book together is more fun than browsing through a shop bought one, and again involves your child as an equal partner in this literacy business. You can even invent strange creatures, and names to go with them, as Lewis Carroll invented the Jabberwocky (there's a good one for 'j'!). It doesn't matter how long or complicated the word is, so long as it begins with the proper sound. You are doing the writing, so your child doesn't have to worry about that, and he will have no trouble remembering what the word says, if he has helped to devise it. Written language isn't just something 'out there', that other and cleverer people have made, but something he can create and generate himself: he can experience the intense delight of being an author, as well as a reader, from the start.

If you are working with an older child, it is even more important to involve him as an 'author' when you tackle the alphabet. The very first step on the way to breaking down the spelling barrier is to learn how to 'tally the bits', but older children with literacy problems are naturally sensitive about their difficulties, and it's easy for them to feel diminished by the suggestion that they should go back and re-learn their letters. There are two ways around this. One is that you don't teach the alphabet at all! Well you do, but not so that your child notices. You simply make sure that as you tally words for him and with him (see the following section), you include all the separate letter-sounds. He probably knows many of them already – it's just that his awareness is patchy, and you need to fill in the gaps. Another way is to ask him to help you make an alphabet book for a younger child in the family – or a cousin – or a neighbour. This is a good plan because it helps him to feel knowledgeable and important in an area where he has been at a disadvantage. Choose a grown up vocabulary to go with the letters – e.g.:

a	astronaut	n	nucleus
b	battleship	o	oxygen
c	computer	p	programme
d	dragon	q	quarter
e	electricity	r	robot
f	flying saucer	s	snake
g	galaxy	t	television
h	helicopter	u	umbrella
i	ink	v	video
j	jet engine	w	witch
k	kilogram	x	x-ray
l	laser	y	yeti
m	microchip	z	zebra crossing

You can teach the combinations in the same way, as if they were single letters. (The combination can come at the beginning of a word, or within it.) Teach both sounds for 'oo' and 'ow', or just the more common one; it doesn't matter. Make a 'Book of Combinations' with your child, this time printing the combination in a bright contrasting colour, in the word, and by itself on the opposite page. E.g.:

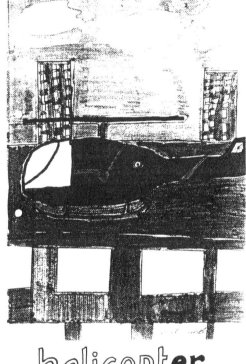

Here is a vocabulary you could use with a young child:

a i	tr<u>ai</u>n	or	m<u>or</u>ning
a y	cr<u>ay</u>on	ew	<u>jew</u>els
au	astron<u>aut</u>	ng	ki<u>ng</u>
a w	p<u>aw</u> or cl<u>aw</u>	oa	b<u>oa</u>t
ch	<u>ch</u>air, <u>ch</u>ildren or ostri<u>ch</u>	oo	br<u>oo</u>m and b<u>oo</u>k
e a	b<u>ea</u>ch	ou	h<u>ou</u>se

ee	queen	ow	cow and elbow
er	hammer, ladder or mother	ph	alphabet or elephant
ir	bird	sh	fish
ur	nurse	th	clothes
ar	car	ui	fruit

and with an older child:

ai	chain	or	port
ay	crayon	ew	jewels
au	astronaut	ng	king
aw	claw	oa	coal
ch	microchip	oo	Typhoo and book
ea	beach	ou	mouth
ee	queen	ow	tower and elbow
er	helicopter	ph	phone or graph
ir	third	sh	shampoo or shadow
ur	nurse	th	third
ar	starboard	ui	fruit

You will notice that I have used some words twice, and also repeated some words from the alphabet list. This is helpful as it enables your child to see that he can tally several different bits in the same word.

As you compile your 'Book of Combinations', read the words and tally the sounds on all the pages you have included so far. By the time the book is completed, your child will feel he was born knowing the sounds for the combinations.

Whenever you wish, refer to your alphabet book to teach the letter names for the five vowels, the consonants c and g – and any other letters you feel like including. By now, though, your child has probably beaten you to this information, just by listening to adults and other children talking about the letters!

VII

Phonic translation

While he is learning all this – before he has learned any of this – after he has learned everything – it doesn't matter – you can begin showing him how to make use of these associations: how to tally the bits so as to tally whole words.

Bear in mind certain points:

1. 'Tallying the bits' has nothing whatever to do with real reading, which is a matter of seeing meanings in patterns of shapes. Carry on helping him to do that by reading all manner of irresistible books to him and with him.
2. Your child can learn to read aloud perfectly competently without 'tallying the bits', by using the 'meaning' bridge between print and speech.
3. More than anything, you are laying the groundwork for confident and accurate spelling, later on.
4. Begin with the whole written word, the whole spoken word, and show your child how to fit them together. This means that you can, if you want, demonstrate the procedure with long and complicated words right from the start: umbrella, helicopter, Jabberwocky. But the first time you encourage your child to copy you, it is probably a good idea to choose something fairly short and simple: 'frog', for instance.
5. As the procedure becomes established, make a point of using it with 'irregular' words as well as regular ones. This will help your child to remember how to spell them.
6. Your child doesn't have to be able to 'work out' words independently, straight away. You are going to show him how to do it, by doing it for

29

him and with him at first. He will later progress quite smoothly to the point where he can do it with unfamiliar words, on his own.

7. With an older child, introduce the technique as an aid to spelling rather than reading. It then strikes him as a more 'grown up' procedure, and once he's mastered it, he will discover himself how effective it can be when he is reading. This happened dramatically for one eleven year old boy I was helping. He brought his maths work card to me, pop-eyed with excitement, indicating a word in tiny print at the top. "Miss – does that word say 'objectives'?" "My goodness Dean, yes it does." Later that morning he dashed up with his reading book. "Miss, Miss – does this word say 'avalanche'? Is that 'distant'? Is that 'rumbling'?" And then, triumphantly, "I worked them all out the way you showed me!"

You can make a start as soon as your child is comfortable about reading aloud, and clearly enjoys it. He has probably noticed certain individual letters, and asked you about them. One day, when he has read a few sentences back to you, choose a shortish, interesting, regular word and tally it for him. "Shall I show you something clever we can do with this word 'frog'?" Cover all the letters, except the 'f', with a thumb or finger. "Look, now it says 'fu'." Uncover the 'r'. "Now it says 'fru'." Uncover the 'o'. "Now it says 'frŏ'." Uncover the 'g'. "Now it says 'frog' again. Isn't that crafty! You have a go – I'll uncover the letters for you." Say the sounds again, and encourage him to say them after you. If he gets in a bit of a muddle, just repeat the sound correctly, and let him have another try. (Marvellous speech therapy, this is!) Then he should tally the word on his own, covering and uncovering the letters himself. When he comes out at the end with both words firmly matched, praise him enthusiastically. "That was marvellous! That was really good! Aren't we clever!"

Tallying one word a day in this manner is quite enough to give him the idea, and once the technique is familiar, it is often fun to help him to use it with the longest and most amazing word you can find. Then he will feel quite flushed with success.

When you reach a combination, simply uncover both letters at once, adding on the next sound. E.g. 'claw' would go 'cu, clu, claw'. The first few times you tackle words containing combinations, it's a good idea to help him identify the combination before you start, so that he's expecting it. "Oh look – this word's got an 'ou' in it, shall we do this one? Pu, pru, prou, proud. Piece of cake!" The idea, in fact, is that you add on just one sound at a time, no matter how many letters it tallies with. 'Through' tallies with 'thu, thrŭ, throo' and 'fright' with 'fu, frŭ, frī, frīt'. Very occasionally it is more convenient to add on two sounds at once. E.g. add 'un' to 'fright' for 'frighten', or 'off' to the 'cu' sound, for 'cough'. Use your own judgement, but try not to add on more than one sound, as the 'one at once' procedure is the most effective way of helping your child to tally all the bits.

When you move on to include 'magic e' words (see Section IX), build them up in a similar fashion. 'Kite' goes 'ku, kĭ, kĭt – kite', or 'clothes' would say 'cu, clu, clŏ, clŏth, clōthe, clothes'.

You can tally the same word for several days in a row, if you wish. Pause for a moment to examine the sheer amount of learning that results just from analysing 'frog'. For your child is now using yet another mathematical procedure, quite naturally – he is operating with *sets*. The written word 'frog' contains, not just four different shapes, but *ten*. Have a look:

f, fr, fro, frog
r, ro, rog
o, og
g

He is taking note of all these permutations and combinations, and the more he practises with 'frog', the more readily he will notice the same sets of letters in other words. For example:

f, fr, fro, frog	frighten, frame, from, frost, froth, froggy
r, ro, rog	rot, romp, cross, grot, grog
o, og	hog, log, bog, dog

as well as any words that contain the single letters 'f', 'r', 'o', 'g'! When you are reading together, you can start to draw his attention to familiar sets of letters. "Oh look – that word 'frosty' has a 'fro' in it, just like 'frog' – and there's an 'og' in 'soggy'." He will soon start pointing them out to you himself.

If he notices the 'ro' in 'brother', you can tackle that word unabashed. 'Bu – bru – bru' again, as the 'o' emerges, 'bruth – bruther'. "Why doesn't it say 'brother', Mum?" "Well, letters don't always go with the same sounds, do they? Most of the time they do, but sometimes they feel like a change." Later, he will remember the apparent 'irregularity', and spell the word correctly.

If you are introducing the procedure as an aid to spelling, choose together a word your child can easily read and say aloud, but has trouble remembering how to spell; tally it, and then help him to spell it back to you. (See Book Three.)

Notice all the advantages of this approach to phonic analysis. Your child's reading is not being held back while he learns to operate the technique – it is continuing apace on a different plane altogether. Then, building up the sounds as you go is much more helpful than saying the sounds separately – fu, ru, o, gu – which bears little resemblance to the finished word. Adding on the sounds means that when the child gets to the end of the written word, he has said the whole spoken word.

But most important of all is what you are *not* doing. *You are not teaching your child that this is an activity at which it is possible to fail.* On the contrary, you are showing him all the time how easy it is, and how brilliant he is at it. You simply don't allow him to get it wrong. So he is encouraged to try out his new found skill more and more – to tackle more and more words – to do it even with words like 'supercalifragilistic-expialidocious' because he knows he can, because it is a supercalifragilisticexpialidociously clever thing to do.

And in the doing of it, elated by his own prowess, he will spend more and more time in the magic world of books, exploring them, getting to know them, taking possession of that world, because it belongs to him by right.

VIII

'Irregular' words

They don't exist!

What has happened is that we have assumed only spoken language is 'real' language – the fixed point of reference at the centre of the universe. Written words, we have also assumed, are just pictures of speech, designed to be a faithful reflection of its every wrinkle, and never supposed to go off and do something different. The point of a phonetic written language is its detailed match with speech – isn't it?

Once we begin to realize that that is by no means the point, we can also begin to think differently about 'irregular' words. The pattern of shapes 'cough' conveys the idea of a noisy chest spasm, just as directly as the pattern of sounds 'coff'. The child can associate the written word with the spoken word by way of the common meaning, and he can also appreciate the phonetic match, linking the 'cu' sound with the letter 'c', and the 'off' sound with 'ough'.

The phonetic bridge between written words and spoken words is indeed convenient, because it allows for a regular traffic flow of meaning, in either direction, between the two forms. But all our solemn pronouncements about the complexities of English spelling, and the difficulties caused by 'irregular' words, show that we have forgotten one very simple fact. *Language is magic.* Give it form and substance, breathe life into it, and it starts to behave as if it had a mind of its own.Written words are spelt the way they are because *they do things that spoken words cannot do.* Or, cannot do so easily, anyway.

One of those things is to bear witness to their historical origin. The dynamism of spoken language means that it is constantly changing. Regional variations in pronunciation crystallize into different dialects, sounds are varied and contracted to make words easier to say at speed. But once written words are recorded on the page, they change their forms much more slowly. There isn't the same drive towards alteration and modification. Today, we can still understand what Shakespeare wrote, although we would probably have great difficulty in following one of his plays if it was presented in its Elizabethan spoken form.

So it is much easier to appreciate the ancestry of written words. The links with the Norse gods of legend are there in 'Wednesday', with its echoes of 'Woden's day', although the spoken word has forgotten all about that, prosaically assuming that its purpose is merely to identify one of the days of the week. We have already noted that a word like 'Worcestershire' stubbornly reminds us that it refers to a *shire*, and that at one time there must have been a Roman camp at a place called 'Wor'. Prefixes and suffixes indicate bonds of meaning between written words that have vanished from the spoken equivalents – look at 'pre-determine' and 'pre-judice', 're-cycle' and 're-turn'. The link between 'mnemonic' and 'amnesia' – from Mnemosyne, the Greek goddess of memory – is there in the spelling, but not in the saying.

Different spellings can also distinguish between the meanings of words which sound exactly the same: 'there' and 'their'; 'hear' and 'here'; 'rain' and 'reign'. The usage of these pairs is usually distinct, but 'aural', for instance, shows that it has a different meaning from 'oral', even though confusion is very likely with the spoken forms, as both words are adjectives, and used in similar contexts.

The strength of our written language lies in the very fact that it can be 'irregular' when it needs to be, and doesn't have to sneeze each time the spoken language catches cold. If we decided to heed Sir James Pitman's strictures, and pin the written language to every nuance of its sister form, we should also remember that it's 'forms', in the plural – and which of those forms would we choose? Our written language, when you think about it, has many of the advantages of an ideographic language. Everybody in England can learn to understand it, despite the variations in speech. Peoples all over the world, whose inheritance of the English tongue has developed into a multiplicity of what are virtually new languages, can nevertheless communicate with one another by means of the written form they hold in common.

'Irregular' words can be read just as easily as any others. (They may be mispronounced – so what?) They can also be spelt just as easily, once a child has taken note of their 'phonetic match'. Their spelling *does* pose problems for dyslexic children, because dyslexics have difficulty in visualizing words accurately, and therefore tend to rely on spelling words 'the way they sound'. But there is a way around this barrier as well. Certainly it doesn't warrant the wholesale abandonment of all the rich cargo of meaning and association that written words have accumulated, over the years, and a flight to the apparent refuge of the 'ita' and similar monstrosities.

Anyway, someone who can seriously call a story in a child's book 'Granny in the Cuntry'[6] just has no soul – and no idea that children see the written forms of language in many other places besides the confines of the printed page.

Footnote

6. See the ita version of *lucky dip*. by Ruth Ainsworth (Puffin).

IX

Getting ready to spell – with alphabet magic

We have seen that because letters are not sounds, they behave in ways that are unavailable to sounds. They have their own dynamics, their own laws. You can have 'silent' letters in words, which nevertheless have very important functions to perform;[7] and many words have double letters, which again are there for a purpose. In order to be able to spell words accurately and confidently, a child needs to understand why letters behave the way they do. This is not a matter of memorizing sets of spelling 'rules', so as to work out the spellings of unfamiliar words. It is a matter of observing certain principles at work in certain familiar words, so that he can remember how to spell them, and notice other words where the same principles are operating.

All he needs to know is a little 'alphabet magic'. If you tell him the story of alphabet magic while he is learning to match words phonetically, he is likely to have few problems with spelling when he starts to generate written words himself. Ideas about magic come naturally to all children, especially young ones; but even thirteen year olds have been known to listen, absorbed, to the tale of the Alphabet Wizard and his problems with the quarrelsome vowels – at least when they think that no one else is eavesdropping! If you are working with a youngster who is not sufficiently confident of his own dignity to relish a bit of magic, you will just have to talk in serious and scientific fashion about 'analysing' words. Try him out first, though – you may be surprised. Many older children love the fantasy world of hobbits, dungeons and dragons, and are so desperate about their spelling that they are quite willing to accept, with relief, anything that helps to make sense of the whole baffling business.

You can begin the story of alphabet magic at any stage of the journey, but the best time is when you want to explain to your child about the workings of the 'magic e'.

Once he has learned to tally words, you can show him how to use the procedure to help him when he is taking his turn at reading back to you. If he is stumped by a word, say, "Well let's try tallying it, and see if that works." Uncover the word yourself, bit by bit, helping him to build up the sounds – and hey presto, there it is. Encourge him to tally the word again, by himself, and then he should re-read the whole sentence, so he can see how the word fits snugly into its written context. (You will soon be able to say, "Tally the word in your head," and he just looks at it 'sternly', moving an imaginary thumb along it.) One day, one of the words you want to tally is going to be a 'magic e' word – for example, cake, bite, hope or tube.

Before that day comes, you need to introduce him to the five vowels, the consonants, and the Alphabet Wizard. Here is the story. Naturally you don't tell him the entire story all at once – just enough to be going on with.

The mighty vowels

'It all begins with the five vowels – a, e, i, o and u – which are the most powerful letters in the alphabet. They go with 'open' sorts of sounds – your mouth is more open when you say the vowels than when you say the other letters. Inside bits of your mouth usually touch each other at some point when you are saying the other letters, which are called consonants. (Try it.) Vowels have certain privileges which most of the consonants don't have – their real letter names, long, spreading out sounds, are quite different from their sound names, which are short and snappy, as in măd, rĕd, bĭt, hŏp, tŭb. So they feel most superior about having two separate sounds to their names. Six consonants (c, g, h, r, w and y) have been given the same privilege, but all the rest of the letters make do with having alphabet names and sound names which are very much alike. But the main reason the vowels tend to throw their weight around, is that although there are only five of them, every single word in the language has *got* to have a vowel in it somewhere.'

If your child is intrigued by this, and promptly begins checking, to see if you are speaking the truth, he will probably emerge triumphant with words like 'my' and 'sky', where there is not a single vowel to be seen. "You're wrong, Mum – look at these words, they don't have any vowels."

'Y' to the rescue

'Well, interesting you should notice that – because what happened was that 'i', who is *supposed* to be the vowel in those words, just lost her nerve when she had to stand at the very end of a word. She felt as if she was at the edge of a precipice, with nothing in front of her, and she had dreadful dizzy turns – vertigo, I suppose you would call it. Her big brothers and sister, 'a', 'o' and 'u', poked fun at her most unkindly, which made her want to run away and hide. Although most of the vowels thought of themselves as 'top people', and wouldn't have much to do with the consonants, 'i' had made friends with 'y', who was flattered to be taken notice of, and went round with her quite a lot. When he saw how upset she was about having to be stuck out at the ends of words, 'y' suggested they should go along to the Alphabet Wizard, and see if he could help. (As a matter of fact, 'y' was a little envious of the vowels, and thought there might be something in it for him.)

'The Alphabet Wizard was the one who had given all their jobs to the letters, in the first place; so if there were any problems he had to try to sort them out. He was a very sympathetic sort of wizard, and understood immediately when 'i' explained about her fears. He didn't believe in making anyone do anything they really didn't want to do. "I tell you what, then, 'i', your friend 'y' seems like a nice considerate sort of chap – and his name sounds very much like yours – why don't we let him do your job, just at the ends of words?"

'"Y' was delighted with that idea, but 'i' was a bit doubtful, at first. "Do you really think so, Wizard – after all, he isn't a *vowel*."

'"He is if I say so," huffed the Wizard. "He can be an *honorary* vowel, just when he's doing your job at the ends of words. We can't ask any of the other vowels to do it, there'd be an awful muddle. I think it's a good plan –

39

you're not doing very much at the moment, are you, 'y'?"

'"No sir – mostly at the beginnings of words, sir, like 'young' or 'yellow'. I'd be glad to help out, sir."

'"All right, that's settled then." So that is why words with an 'ĭ' or 'ī' sound at the end almost always end in 'y' – 'donkey', 'baby', 'library', 'fry' and so on. And there are hardly any words that end in 'i'. One or two, because the thing about alphabet magic is that it never works all the time – there are always some gaps in it somewhere. I'll give you five pence for every different word ending in 'i' you can find, apart from proper names.' ('Genii, 'ski', 'pi' and 'ti', which is a kind of Polynesian tree, are the only ones I can think of, so that is a fairly safe offer, and may well encourage your child to start exploring the dictionary!)

'I felt as if she was at the edge of a precipice'

The magic 'e'

'The next problem happened with the 'e', who was the littlest of the vowels, even though he came second in alphabetical order. 'E's difficulty was that he couldn't talk very well. Sometimes he could manage a squeak, but most of the time, no matter how hard he tried, opening his mouth wide

40

and gathering all his breath together, he just couldn't get anything to come out at all. He became vey upset – and once again 'a' 'o' and 'u' made his life a misery because of it. Finally he got in such a mood that he insisted on plonking himself down in as many words as he could – and not saying anything. That made 'a' 'o' and 'u' even more angry, and they grumbled at him all the time. 'I' didn't, because she knew what it felt like to be made fun of for something you couldn't help. At last, seeing how upset he was, she took him off to the Alphabet Wizard. 'Y' came too because it made him feel important.

'Once again, the Alphabet Wizard was very sympathetic. He didn't like letters who were horrible to other letters, and felt they should be put in their place. "I don't see why you have to say anything at all, if you don't feel like it, 'e'," he declared. "Far too much gabbing and shouting as it is. Very nice to have a fellow like yourself who can keep his mouth shut from time to time. But those brothers and sisters of yours need to be taught a lesson. Now, let me think. Got it! I will give to you, 'e' – and only to you, because I've taken a shine to you – the most powerful magic there is." 'E' could hardly wait, he was so excited. "This magic is," said the Alphabet Wizard very slowly, getting it out of an old dusty box, "the power to make your fellow beings *say their names*." 'E' was a bit disappointed, because it didn't sound all that marvellous, but the Alphabet Wizard explained. "If you can make someone else tell you his name, then he is forever in your power. All the other magic there is begins with the 'naming' spell. So it's very important magic, 'e', and you must use it carefully. You can work it in the words where you don't feel like saying anything yourself. I'll arrange things so that it only affects the other vowels, making them say their alphabet names – 'i' as well, I'm afraid, otherwise there would be an awful muddle." The Wizard had a thing about muddles. "And you too, 'e' – you will have to make other 'e's' say their names. It will work through one consonant, but not through two. Will that help?"

'Well, the 'e' and the 'i', not forgetting the 'y', decided that would do nicely, and off they went. So that is why 'm-a-d' says 'mad' – but 'm-a-d-e' says 'made'. 'Bit' turns into 'bite', 'hop' turns into 'hope' and 'tub' turns into 'tube'. There aren't many words where the magic works on an 'e' coming earlier in the word, because 'e' felt a bit silly, working the magic on himself; 'these' and 'scene' are two examples, though.

'I' and 'y' join in

'Everything went along swimmingly for a time, but of course there was another problem. There always is. The Alphabet Wizard kept hoping he'd sorted everything out, but once you've set alphabet magic to work, you can never quite foresee all the snags. What happened next was that a great many words realized how useful the 'e's' new magic power actually was. There were masses of them needing vowels to say their alphabet names, and poor little 'e' was rushed off his feet. All the other letters could go off on their holidays from time to time, basking in the sun at Majorca, but 'e' didn't have time to put his feet up for a tea break, even, let alone skip away to Majorca. He began to look so pale and wretched that 'i' and 'y' whisked him up and went back to see the Alphabet Wizard.

'By this time the Alphabet Wizard was beginning to feel just a bit exasperated, but he tried not to show it. After all, 'e' really didn't look well. "All *right*, 'e'," he snapped, and then he smiled. "Poor old thing, you do need a rest, don't you. Doing your job too wholeheartedly, that's the trouble. We'll have to give you a stand-in for some of the time. Now let me see – trouble is, we can't let the consonants work magic, that isn't allowed. The Magicians' Union would be down on me like a ton of bricks. It will have to be one of the other vowels."

' 'I' tried to look extremely conscientious and helpful at this point, and it worked. "How about you, 'i'? You wouldn't mind standing in for the 'e' every now and then, would you? Good, that's settled then."

' "Er – just a moment, sir," put in 'y', feeling desperately excited. "Aren't you forgetting something? I do the 'i's job sometimes, don't I. So I – that is me, 'y', of course – I will have to be allowed to work the magic too."

' "Certainly not," said the Wizard crossly. "Can't have that – you're not a proper vowel. I'd get into awful trouble."

' "I am a vowel if you say so, sir," pointed out the 'y', smoothly hoisting the Wizard with his own petard. "I'm an *honorary* vowel – you said so yourself."

'The Alphabet Wizard could see that he wouldn't have any peace until he agreed, so he gave in. "All right, all right, all *right*. Both of you can do it, when the 'e' needs a break. Now – be off with you. *I* need a rest after all this."

So that is the reason, when you want to add an ending beginning with 'i' or 'y' to a 'magic e' word, that the 'e' goes off and puts his feet up, and the 'i' (or the 'y') does the 'e's magic job for him. 'Hope' turns into 'hoping'; 'shine' turns into 'shining' or 'shiny'; 'bone' and 'shake' turn into 'bony' and 'shaky'. Keep a look out for the words where the 'e' is having a rest – there are quite a lot. But of course when you want to add an ending beginning with a *consonant*, like 'f' or 'l' – they're not allowed to use magic, so the 'e' has to stay. 'Hope' becomes 'hopeful' or 'hopeless', 'use' becomes 'useful' and 'useless'. 'A', 'o' and 'u' were not allowed to share in the magic power, either, to begin with – notice 'likeable' – although 'a' and 'u' became involved to some extent later, as we shall see.

The double defence

'You would think that by now everybody would be happy – but not a bit of it. In no time at all the Wizard was being pestered again, and not just by one or two letters. This time the words were up in arms. The trouble was that 'i' and 'y' were so enormously pleased with themselves for being able to share in the 'e's magic powers, they took their jobs just as seriously as he did. They all insisted on working the magic at every possible opportunity. So when 'trot' wanted an 'ing' ending, the 'i' promptly got to work on the 'ŏ' sound – and the word didn't *say* 'trotting' at all, but 'trōting'! 'Web' wanted an 'ed' ending, and was made to say 'weebed' instead of 'webbed', and 'mud' turned all 'moody' instead of 'muddy'. Talk about confusion! The Wizard had plenty of muddle on his hands now, all right. He was so cross when he discovered all the words squawking and squabbling on his

43

doorstep, he banged the door on the lot of them and shouted through a window. "Look – I told you! Sort it out yourselves. The single defence won't work, but the double defence will." Then he went off on his own holidays, to the Bahamas, through the back door.

'The words stared at each other blankly. What could he mean? It was the 'e' who remembered. "I know, I know," he squeaked, finding his voice in a rush, "it'll work through one consonant, but *not through two.* You've got to double your last consonant, trot – and web – and mud – then we can't work our magic on you! Tro<u>tt</u>ing, you see – and we<u>bb</u>ed – and mu<u>ddy</u>! Piece of cake!"

'Well of course he was quite right. After a bit of grumbling among themselves, the words had to agree that he was right, and double their final consonants if they wanted to protect the short and snappy vowel sounds against the powers of the 'e', 'i' and 'y'. Long words didn't always bother, feeling that they had enough muscle anyway, but just about all the short ones did, and were glad of the nice safe feeling it gave them to be tucked away behind their doubled consonants, when the 'e', 'i' or 'y' were on the warpath. See how many 'doubly defended' words you can find – there are masses of them.

The single defence won't work . . .
. . . but the double defence will.

Cees and gees and the bodyguard 'u'

'The interesting thing was that the odd bit of alphabet magic kept emerging and 'doing its own thing' even after the Wizard had gone away in disgust. The vowels, feeling they were 'top people', tried to bring it under control and deal with it sensibly, but they didn't do a very good job. The Wizard had intended for the 'naming' magic to affect only the vowels, but after a while a strange thing happened. Two of the consonants whose alphabet names were quite different from their sound names, 'c' and 'g', discovered that whenever an 'e' , 'i' or 'y' came immediately after them in a word, they began to say just the *beginnings* of their names. Look at 'ceiling', 'city', 'cygnet'; 'gentle', 'giant' and 'gypsy'. 'A', 'o' and 'u', of course, had no effect, as in 'cold', 'case', 'cuckoo'; 'gold', 'gas', 'gut'. But, the magic, since it was only stray, wandering around sort of magic, didn't work all the time, particularly with 'g', as you can see in words like 'get', 'girl' or 'give'. Nevertheless, it still caused a few headaches. The words 'g-ess' and 'g-ide' found themselves saying 'jess' and 'jide', which was a nuisance. What was to be done? 'A' declared scornfully it was obvious, you just had to double the 'g', as the Wizard had said. 'E' pointed out with a superior smirk that that wouldn't work at all – the magic would simply affect the *second* 'g'. If 'a' would have a look at 'accident', for example, he would see what 'e' meant. 'C' was all right, because 'k' could protect him when necessary, as in the words 'lucky', 'cracked' and 'rocking' – but 'g' was a different matter. No other consonant made a 'gu' sound, so who could do the job? "One of us vowels will have to do the defending this time," decided the 'e'. "It had better be 'u' – he keeps grumbling he doesn't have any important jobs." However, 'u' was not best pleased to be appointed bodyguard to a mere consonant, and wriggled out of it whenever he could. So he turns up in 'guess', 'guest', 'guide' and 'guile', but as we've seen, he doesn't bother for 'get', 'girl' and 'give' – among others. And sometimes, just to be really awkward, he plonks himself down in words where he isn't needed at all, like 'guard' and 'guarantee'. The Wizard was horrified by the muddle the letters had made, when he got back from his holidays, but it was really his fault for going away and leaving them to it. Anyway, he should have known that you could never be quite sure of anything, with alphabet magic.'

Although certain aspects of this tale are self evident, particularly where it concerns the workings of the magic 'e', some of the principles involved are not at all obvious, even to quite experienced readers. Many children (and adults!) have no idea why the 'e' is dropped from 'bony' and 'shining'; or why the consonants have to be doubled in words such as 'muddy', 'batted' and 'sobbing'; or what the 'u' is doing in 'guess' and 'guide'. (Often they know there is supposed to be a 'u' there somewhere, but just where and why is another matter.) The point about explaining the effects of 'alphabet magic' is not that the 'magic' is totally reliable – we have just seen that it isn't. But it helps a child to understand why a great many words are spelled the way they are: it arouses his interest in the structure of words, and the whys and wherefores of their spelling. As he begins to follow through all the twisting ways the magic works, until he can spot the words where the magic *should* be working, but isn't, so his ability to spell both 'obedient' and 'disobedient' words becomes increasingly confident. Accurate spelling results simply from looking at words in an interested and analytical way, and it is this way of looking at words which is fostered by the story of the Alphabet Wizard and the unruly letters.[8]

I don't tell the whole story to adolescents, but bits of it come in handy, when explaining the 'double defence' system, for instance. I give all my students the following summary of the 'six magic spells', and explain the principles involved as examples occur. The rules are written out here in cursive handwriting (which I'll say a lot more about in Book Three). Please feel free to photocopy the list.

With a much younger child, you have all the time in the world. If the story unfolds while you are exploring books together, then later, when he is making written words himself, he will find the spellings naturally and readily at his fingertips, as if they have come by magic.

As, indeed, they have.

Footnotes

7. The prime function of the silent 'e' is to affect the *meaning* of a word; e.g. by changing 'hop' to 'hope'! Modifying the vowel sound is a secondary consideration.

8. The principles of 'alphabet magic' are easier to grasp if the magic power is seen as limited to 'e' 'i' and 'y'. (This explains 'likeable' and 'traceable', and why words like 'gate' 'gold' and 'gun' do not need to protect their 'gu' sounds.) Very occasionally, though, in some longer words like 'unmistakable' or 'forgettable', the 'a' is allowed to take part, here doing the 'e's magic job, or needing to be guarded against. There is no need to include this as part of the story, but when examples crop up, you can point out what is happening, explaining that the 'a' repented of his earlier unkind attitude towards the 'e', and quite enjoyed wielding the magic power himself from time to time!

SIX MAGIC RULES

(How to become a magician, and learn to <u>spell</u>.)

1. ## <u>The magic 'e' spell</u>

    Magic 'e' has the power to <u>make a vowel say its name</u>.

    E.g.   mad   made
            bit   bite
            hop   hope
            us   use

2. ## <u>The magic 'i' and magic 'y' spell</u>

    Sometimes magic 'e' needs a tea-break. Then he chooses two other vowels, 'i' or 'y' (which can sometimes work as a vowel), to do his magic job for him.

    So if you want to add an ending to a magic 'e' word, and the ending begins with 'i' or 'y', <u>drop the 'e'</u> first.

    E.g. <u>shine</u> becomes shin<u>i</u>ng or shin<u>y</u>

3. ## <u>Consonants can't use magic</u>

    Consonants are <u>not allowed</u> to use magic. (They don't belong to the Magicians' Union.)

    So if you want to add an ending to a magic 'e' word, and the ending begins with a <u>consonant</u> the 'e' has to stay to do his magic job.

    E.g. hope becomes hop<u>e</u>ful or hop<u>e</u>less.

4. ## <u>The double defence system</u>

    Sometimes you need to protect the short vowel sounds against the magic vowels. E.g. 'trot'. If you just added 'ing', it would say 'troting'.

    So double the final consonant before adding an ending beginning with 'e', 'i' or 'y'.

E.g.　trot　　trotting
　　　　mud　　muddy
　　　　web　　webbed

(If the short vowel sound in the original word is followed by two consonants anyway – e.g. mi<u>lk</u>, lu<u>ck</u>, du<u>st</u> – then it's already protected, and the magic vowels can't get at it: mi<u>lk</u>ing, lu<u>ck</u>y, du<u>st</u>er.)

5. <u>Changing 'c's and 'g's</u>

The magic vowels can make <u>c</u>'s and g's say <u>just</u> <u>the</u> <u>beginnings</u> <u>of</u> <u>their</u> <u>names</u>. They have to come right after the c or the g to do this.
E.g. ceiling, city, cygnet;　gentle, giant, gypsy

A's, o's and u's cannot work this magic. So: cold, case, cuckoo;　gold, gas, gut

Because c's and g's are <u>consonants</u>, the magic is more difficult to do. Sometimes it doesn't work – notice 'give', 'get', 'girl', etc.

6. <u>The bodyguard 'u'</u>

If the hard 'g' sound thinks he needs defending, he hides behind a bodyguard 'u' which protects him from the magic vowels.
E.g. guess, guide, plague, guy

Sometimes bodyguard 'u' gets fed up (because he isn't allowed to work magic himself, even though he's a vowel). So he plonks down in words where he isn't really needed. Just to be awkward!
E.g. guard, guarantee

<u>REMEMBER</u> – the magic vowels work properly most of the time, but sometimes their spells go wrong. (Everybody has an off day from time to time.) Look out for the words where the magic <u>doesn't</u> work – this will help you to remember how to spell them.

X

Ways around the barriers

a) Deafness

Of course you cannot teach phonic translation to a totally deaf child.

Or, if you could, there wouldn't be much point, because he can't hear words, so 'hearing shapes' is an impossibility.

Remember that nothing in this literacy business is quite what it seems. It is true that a totally deaf child cannot learn to 'hear shapes'. *But he can learn to say them.*

It won't help him to read. It will help him to talk.

If you have a deaf child, and you want to help him to talk, first think through in your own mind the processes that a hearing baby has to follow when he learns to talk.

It all starts when he is about five months old, and begins to babble. There he is, stuck in his cot with nothing much to do. He's exhausted the possibilities of his rattle and his mobile, and he can't go exploring as he hasn't yet perfected the crawl. Life is looking distinctly boring, when it dawns on him that he has a custom made plaything literally under his nose. As he waggles his lips and tongue, these rather interesting noises come out.

To begin with, he probably doesn't realize that he is producing the sounds himself. But quite soon he notices that the same sounds happen whenever he has the same feelings in his mouth and voice. This is a very exciting discovery. It means that he can produce sounds at will. When he pulls his lips apart, with a bit of voice behind them, a rather nifty 'bu' sound emerges. And if he does it again, the *same thing* happens! Very satisfying. Waggling things around at the back of his throat produces a nice 'gooey' sound, and there seem to be all sorts of things he can do with his tongue. Perhaps life has possibilities after all.

Does anything about this process strike you as familiar? What the baby is doing is *tallying*! He is linking the feelings of producing sounds (we could call them 'vocal sensations') with the heard sounds that come through his ears. Only when these associations have been firmly made can he begin to imitate sounds. His mother leans over his cot, going 'ba – ba – ba' in the inane way mothers have, and he finds this delightful because the sounds his mother is making *are just like the sounds he has already learned to make himself.* (His mother, at first, is imitating him!) So he can go 'ba – ba – ba' in reply. The two of them can have a fine old time, going 'ba – ba – ba' and 'gu – gu – gu' at each other for minutes on end. Even better: his babbling game has now spread out to include someone else.

But the sounds the baby is hearing are not just random noises. Some of the patterns of sounds coming through his ears are important to him because he has already learned to associate them with ideas – he has learned to understand them. The pattern of sounds 'Mu-ma' means his mother. One day, it dawns on him that because he too can produce the set of sounds 'Mu-ma' with his own voice, he too can invest that set of sounds with a meaning. *He* can say 'Mu-ma' *and mean his mother.* So he does.

He is not just babbling any longer. Now, he is speaking.

Once a child realizes that he can generate words of his own, the whole undertaking opens out into vistas of delight. Things around him have names, and uttering their names gives him a triumphant sense of possession over them. Some of these names he can say quite easily, because he has already learned them as random utterances when he was playing with his voice. But if he hears a word he has not yet produced by chance, another process comes into operation. He has learned all the separate sounds used by speakers of his native tongue, during the babbling stage. (In fact he has uttered all the sounds available to the human voice, of whatever tongue. But he repeats only those sounds reflected back to him by other voices, and jettisons the rest.) Now when he hears a new word he wishes to repeat himself, he has to listen to it very carefully and analytically. He has to isolate the initial sound in the word he hears, and match it with the corresponding vocal sensation. He then has to identify the sound that comes next, and pair that off with the feeling of producing it. And so on, all along the word, until he has achieved a matching set of vocal sensations which re-produces the word he hears.

He has tallied the word he hears with the word he says, and he has used exactly the same intellectual procedure that a reading child uses when he tallies a word he *sees* with a word he says. The hearing baby tallies words because he wants to match them with each other, to translate them. A reading child tallies words because he too wants to translate them into each other. The process is the same.

If a deaf baby learns to tally written words with spoken words, what will it help him to do? It won't help him to read, because he cannot understand the spoken words. But if he has already learned to understand print, then tallying the words he sees *will help him to speak.* He will be able to invest the sounds he produces with the meanings shining through the written words: he can learn to speak by matching meaningful words with his own feelings of utterance. Which is exactly how a hearing child learns to speak.

I am not talking witchcraft here! You may have to think through what I am saying once or twice to see how the process really works. But it involves no revolutionary methodology. All this has been done. Deaf children do learn to understand print without reference to speech. And it is quite possible to teach phonics to a child who is totally deaf. What we haven't done is to grasp *why* these procedures are significant – that when a totally deaf child learns reading and phonics, he is learning to understand and reproduce language *in exactly the same way as a hearing child.* The only difference is, he is using pattens of shapes as his point of reference, the hearing child is using patterns of sounds.

We are all so convinced that 'phonics' is a *reading* method, it just hasn't dawned on us that it is nothing of the kind. It is a translating procedure, pure and simple. And the meanings of words travel in either direction. All *hearing* children who are fluent readers also 'learn to speak' by tallying written words with spoken words! They learn the meanings of new words by reading them, and translate them into spoken words by using the 'phonetic bridge'. We have insisted for decades that a child increases his vocabulary by reading, without pausing to analyse the means whereby this is accomplished, or to recognize the implications for the teaching of literacy. Or to see what it can mean for *deaf* children.

If you have a deaf child, and you want to help him to undestand print, and then to tally print with speech, be assured that he can learn these things very easily. Hearing children can learn them, and a deaf child is only a hearing child who cannot hear. (Mothers of deaf children will know what I mean!) All the difficulties will be on your side, in working out how to make the associations available. Don't give up, don't be discouraged, applaud yourself for every success, and ignore the 'failures'. You cannot fail – your child is learning all the time, and anything the does not learn today he can easily learn tomorrow. Don't worry that what you do may conflict with what your child is learning at school, or with his comprehension of the limited spoken language he can perceive. The more language he is exposed to, of more different kinds, the more he will understand. Hearing children learn both spoken and written language without being confused. Each form of language supplies and enriches the other. Deaf children can learn both languages too. In the reverse order.

Begin by reading, or re-reading, *The Story of My Life,* by Helen Keller. If untrained Anne Sullivan could give the whole world of language to a child who was both blind and deaf, then the world of language is accessible to every child, no matter what his handicap.

Next, review the tallying process. It is a matter of linking two separate items as a pair. You can begin with either item, and then match it with the other one. The two 'items' you want your child to associate are a visual shape, and a particular feeling of utterance. (Notice that you can *feel* the difference between producing varying sounds, whether you can hear those sounds or not.) So, when your child sees the letter 'b', you want him to link the shape with the feeling of going 'bu'.

You cannot do it that way round. So simply reverse the order. Begin with the feeling of utterance, and when that happens, match it as soon as you can with the corresponding set of shapes. Whenever or however your child is persuaded to produce a 'bu' sound, for example,[9] then straightaway show him the letter 'b'. If you help him to make the link several times, you will very soon be able to show him the letter 'b', and *he will respond with the matching sound.* If he produces a 'ba' sound, show him 'ba'. Or a 'bub' sound, show him 'bub'. Do this as much as you can with as many sets of letters as you can (a computer would be ideal for the purpose) and the associations will steadily take root. Don't 'test' your child; just keep on providing the associations. Teach the most common sound for each letter and combination, but also teach the alphabet names for the vowels and the consonants 'c' and 'g'.

When he has clearly formed a reasonable number of links, you can begin helping him to tally words. Again, a computer could provide the most effective means of doing this. Print a word in large clear letters on the screen, and cover it with your thumb or fingers. As you uncover it, encourage your child to produce the matching sound. Say it yourself at the same time so that he can lipread. 'Bed', for instance, would go 'bu, bĕ, bed'. Praise him and encourage him all the time, and tally an increasing number of words each day. He will soon get the idea that this procedure enables him to *say* the words he sees. You can link 'irregular' words with a phonetic version. E.g. print 'cough' on the screen, and then, underneath it, 'say coff' and help your child to tally the second version. After a while he can use the computer by himself, to practise.

At what age should you begin? As young as possible: capitalize on the babbling stage if you are aware of his disability then. Many deaf children babble, but because they don't hear the sounds they make, they don't have any heard sounds with which to link their feelings of utterance. So the babbling stage passes without their learning how to produce sounds at will. An older deaf child has to be taught to produce sounds, but this can be done; it's just a more laborious process.

Think about what you are not doing, as well as what you are. If your child's hearing is very limited, you will not be able to convey the tone, inflection and emphasis of the human voice, and his own speech will necessarily be awkward and approximate in the way that is characteristic of people who have been severely deaf from birth. What you will be enabling him to do is to transfer meanings from the words he sees to the words he says. So that when he talks, he knows what he is saying.

A very exciting step forward in the eduction of deaf children has been the development of 'cued speech'. Cued speech, too, springs from the recognition that since deaf people can see much more easily than they can hear, it makes sense to use their visual perception as a main route to all forms of language.

Deaf people have learned to lipread for generations. The difficulty is that many different sounds 'look' exactly the same on the lips, so both understanding and reproduction of words by the lipreader tends to be imprecise.

Cued speech was devised by Dr Orin Cornett to get over this problem. The hands are used as 'cues' at the side of the face, in conjunction with normal speech, to clear up ambiguities, and make plain exactly which sounds are being uttered. This makes far more complex language accessible to the deaf lipreader, and his own speech can also be corrected by the appropriate use of 'cues'. Deaf children who are exposed to cued speech begin to take real interest in learning to lipread, and once their understanding is fluent, they can lipread more readily even when the speaker is not cueing.

When cued speech has become familiar, you can of course use it to help your child learn to translate written words into sounds. 'Cue' any written words, or letters, that you want him to say, and by this simple means you will enable him to match the shapes on the page with the precisely equivalent 'vocal sensations'.

If you would like more information about cued speech, write to: Mrs June Dixon, Director, The National Centre for Cued Speech, 29/30 Watling Street, Canterbury CT1 2UD. Tel: 0227 450757.

b) Visual defects

Teach the tallying process to a child with visual problems in exactly the same way that you would teach a sighted child. Think of how you would proceed with a totally blind child, and then adapt your approach according to how much your child can see.

A blind child can learn to read and tally, just like a sighted child. The only difference is that the patterns of shapes are felt rather than seen. Help him to understand written words first, and then, within that context, to 'tally the bits' with sounds.

c) Dyslexia

'Tallying the bits' involves an entirely different way of looking at written words from real reading. The first time a child does it with a particular word, it's almost as if he has to change into bottom gear. The flow of meaning is temporarily halted while he stops, shifts the gear lever, brings his focal point smartly forward, and looks at the word 'sternly'. He may have to do this once or twice with the same word, but when the printed and spoken versions are well married, he can take the word in his stride thereafter, without having to change gear to note its phonetic match. It registers, but what matters now is looking through the word as a transparent whole, to the point where the meaning shifts and shimmers.

One fascination about working with a dyslexic child is that this change of gear is particularly marked, magnified many times over, and you can actually watch it happening. (A dyslexic may continue physically covering and uncovering words for a lot longer than other children.) It's important for a dyslexic child to learn to tally the bits, because the procedure offers his only hope of learning to spell confidently. It is equally important to recognize that the procedure is quite useless to him when he is getting going with real reading. What matters then is forming the mental 'cluster' of images for a word (e.g. apple, pelap, alepp, abbel, etc.) and realizing that *they all mean the same thing.* It seems likely that the word on the page, once it is firmly linked to the cluster in the child's head, does come to look like a sort of amalgamation of that cluster (because we see what we expect to see) – and matching sounds to 'pelapp' gets you precisely nowhere, as far as understanding the word is concerned.

A dyslexic faces numerous hurdles on the road to fluent literacy. It is the same road for him that it is for everybody else, but someone has inconsiderately placed all these invisible barriers in his way. What is even more disheartening is that when, with enormous courage and determination, he finally succeeds in blasting his way through the barriers, scratched and bleeding and dripping with sweat, his fellows have the nerve to turn around and try to maintain that the barriers were never there in the first place. "You see," they say smugly, looking straight through the invisible pieces of barrier littering the road, "we told you you could do it if you tried."

Reading is the first hurdle, because of having to learn the meanings of so many different forms of written words. Handwriting is often laboured and untidy, because it's difficult to visualize the way the letters are supposed to look. Spelling is a nightmare for the same reason. If the written word 'apple' can assume as many as five different forms in your head, then it seems sensible to spell it in any one of the same five ways (often all on one page!) – nobody ever *told* you that each and every written word has only one correct spelling, for always and always amen.

The reading hurdle is the easiest to demolish, provided someone realizes what is happening and is prepared to read to you and with you for as long as it takes, indicating the print in a casual and fluent way to help you follow. There is a style of handwriting that is recommended for dyslexics because it can be learned 'by the feel' rather than by having to visualize it. There are word processors and typewriters and tape recorders and nice helpful people called scribes whose job it is to write down the words out of your head, so as to convince you that you are just as much of an author as anybody else.

The spelling barrier is the most fearsome, and the most exasperating: it shouldn't matter, but it does. You may have written your heart out in a story, or a poem, but when other people read what you have written, all they can see are the spelling mistakes. "Correct your spelling mistakes," they say, and you look at them blankly. Spelling mistakes? *What spelling mistakes?*

Learning to 'tally the bits' isn't the whole answer to the spelling problem, but this barrier cannot be broken down without mastery of the tallying technique. If you have any reason to suspect that your child could be dyslexic, make a point of teaching him the sounds for all the letters and combinations, and help him to tally as many different words as possible, especially irregular words. He is likely to confuse left and right, and the physical process of covering the word with his finger, and uncovering it bit by bit, moving his finger to the right, helps him to grasp the difference between these two directions. Do the covering and uncovering for him until he can do it on his own; then gradually encourage him to do it 'just by looking'. The ability to tally is a great confidence booster. It helps the child to feel that he can control written words when he has to. If they are getting out of hand, all he needs to do is to stop and 'look at them sternly', and they will behave themselves again.

Footnote

9 See Sir Alexander and Lady E.C. Ewing, *Teaching Deaf Children to Talk*, Manchester University Press, 1964

XI

Alphabetical order

Your child does not need to recite the alphabet so as to read and to tally, nor does he need to know the alphabet names of all the letters.

Knowing the alphabet names is useful when he is doing oral spelling (see Book Three), and when he wants to talk about the letters to other people in approved grown up fashion. He needs to be able to recite the alphabet when he consults any work of reference that is arranged alphabetically, particularly a dictionary. Or to help him appreciate where he comes in a class list.

Dyslexics often get the alphabet in a hopeless muddle for the same reason that they get words in hopeless muddles: they cannot visualize it accurately. Most people, when they stop to think about it, do visualize the order of the letters. I 'see' the letters going from left to right, in reasonably horizontal fashion, at the bottom of my mind. (Days of the week, though, go from right to left, further up, and, again like many people, I 'see' them in different colours!) You can teach your child the alphabet names of the letters, and their alphabetical order, whenever it seems like a good idea. Bear in mind that a dyslexic child is going to have difficulty with the order of the letters, and you need to give him additional help to keep them straight.

Strong, rhythmic speech patterns are an excellent 'anchor' for a dyslexic. He may not be able to visualize the alphabet, but he can learn to chant it. Conveniently, the alphabet breaks down into neat rhythmic 'chunks':

a b c,	n o p q,
d e f g,	r s t u,
h i,	v w x y z
j k	
l m	

61

Chant the alphabet together when you are going shopping, or doing the washing up, emphasizing the stressed letter in each chunk. (Beat out the rhythm on a few pan lids!) Make up a tune for it if you feel so inclined. You could design a frieze for your child's room, divided into the same groups of letters, illustrating each one, and picking out the stressed letter in red or any other contrasting colour. Show your child how dictionaries, telephone books, encyclopaedias are arranged in alphabetical order, and help him to find words in a dictionary, beginning with words he already knows, and moving on to the strangers later.

He can master all these things 'without really thinking about it'. And as he grows up, letters and words will not be alien, threatening beings, but familiar friends: ready, whenever he wishes, to arrange themselves in a myriad bright patterns, and to march at his command.

THE NATURAL WAY TO LEARN

THE APPRENTICESHIP APPROACH TO LITERACY

BOOK THREE

Generating Written Words

MAKING THINGS
WITH
WORDS AND THINGS

Felicity Craig

CONTENTS BOOK 3

Illustrated by
Edward Dart, Lee Barlow, Ben Kerrison, Lea Humphreys,
Sarah Dart, Barry Dowding, Andrew Hard, Martin Lye,
Lee Berry, Darrell Parkin, Jason Parkin.

I

Why do we write?

Maybe my teachers taught me to write. I don't remember. But it was my father who made me a writer, long before I had any idea of how to put pen to paper. He had been listening to me wittering on one day, and decided, as only a fond parent could, that what I had been saying was not childish prattle at all, but immortal verse. So he sat down at his typewriter, and lo and behold, the words that had come out of my head appeared on the flimsy sheet of typing paper before him, in deep blue print. I can remember the look of the typed words, and the feel of the paper: I can almost remember its smell. The last line in each verse was about twice as long as the others, stretching near to infinity across the page, and declared:

'But best of all I like to see all the birds singing in a tree.'

I hope that I have written a small amount of real poetry since then. But no writing I have formed myself has ever filled me with such an electric sense of wonder and exaltation as that very first sight and feel of my own words in print. They were out there and visible, just like real book words, they were mine, and they would last forever.

Human beings invented language, it is said, so as to communicate with each other. Our purpose was strictly utilitarian. We could tell our fellows the names of herbs and their uses; or what to do when a child fell sick; or where the wild animals were that we needed to catch and eat. Yet this view of the inception of language assumes that some such grand social design impelled us to our very first utterance. We had to invent words because we knew we needed them to survive as a species.

Rubbish. We invented words because we had ideas in our heads. In some mysterious and magical way we found we could make patterns of sounds with our voices that were so closely fused with these ideas that they became the ideas. Something we had formed in our own minds could be felt on our lips and tongues, and vibrate within our ears. We made words because we like making things.

The most marvellous discovery was that these constructs of our minds and voices were somehow 'out there'; not only sounding in our own ears – but our husbands and wives, brothers and sisters, could hear them too. And as these sounds resonated in other ears besides our own, *they carried the ideas with them.* Numinous images that we had supposed unique to ourselves appeared, as if by magic, in other people's minds.[1] 'Communication' happened as a kind of byproduct. Our initial impulse in sharing words was the same which leads us to take a fellow being by the hand and point out to him, with pride, the amazingly beautiful mudpies we have just completed.

For thousands of years, spoken words were enough. Anybody with a functioning voice box could produce them, and anybody with ears and a human mind could understand them. No outside materials were called for. But the trouble was that they had the defects of their qualities. Because they were so immediate, carried on a puff of air, they disappeared as soon as they were uttered; and if you wanted to recreate the same ideas, you had to go to the trouble of uttering them all over again. Clearly something more permanent was needed, if the mudpies were not to be continually washed away.

Generating spoken words did give us the ability to communicate with each other, and so share our tool making and weapon making skills, to build societies and cities, to pass on to our children, in the art of the tale teller, the history of our deeds.

Generating written words made us immortal. We invented ways of making words visible, not really because we wanted to communicate with people beyond our closest reach. Enchanted and intrigued by these fabulous pictures of the ideas inside our heads, we carved them in stone because we wanted them to last forever.

Footnote

1 See Susanne Langer, *Philosophy in a New Key*, p.134.

II

The author in your child

This is why your child needs to learn to write. One day he will have to write that his teachers want, to prove that he is indeed benefiting from his academic studies. He will have to sign cheques and fill in forms, draft his curriculum vitae, compose letters of application. The very first words he makes have nothing to do with any of this. He covers pieces of paper with his earnest childish scrawl because of his wonderful discovery that these words can be seen by anybody, and unlike the words he says, they will last forever. By the end of the day the pieces of paper find their way, unnoticed, to the rubbish bin. It doesn't matter. Once he knows how to do it, tomorrow he can make some more words that will last forever.

At the very start, spelling doesn't matter, the way he holds his pencil doesn't matter, the shapes and sizes of the individual letters signify not a jot. What does matter is that you should celebrate with him his joy and pride in his stupendous achievement. Now he is literate; now he is an author.

Liz Waterland, in a follow up article to *Read With Me, An Apprenticeship Approach to Reading*,[2] points out that the very first step on the road to successful reading is that *the child should realize that books are worthwhile*. Before this, you have nothing; and when you have this, you have everything. If he falls in love with books, you will not be able to stop him.

Similarly, the very first step on the road to successful writing is that the child should experience the glory of seeing his own words written down. So the best way to begin is not by teaching him to form letters. The best way is to do as my father did, and write down for him the words out of his head. Once he has tasted the possibilities, you will not have to teach him to write independently. He will demand to learn

What sort of words does he need to see, written down?

At the heart of language is the act of noticing sameness. Only by

7

identifying the common factors of 'chairs', 'doors' and 'coats', can a child form the concepts which are represented by words. It is by means of this perception of the common form in objects that language spreads and branches. Its basic thrust is not prosaic at all, but poetic: *it grows by means of metaphor*. For the child is noticing 'samenesses' at white heat; scarcely have his words crystallized than he can use them to take tremendous metaphorical leaps. A 'coat' has sleeves and fastenings and is made of cloth, or so you would think, yet all these characteristics can be discarded as he flashes to the essential similarity between a winter overcoat and the new layer of paint on the front door, so that the front door can truly be described as wearing a 'coat' of paint.[3]

Look out, then for his similes and metaphors – they are there for the listening – and write them down. When he is struggling to keep up on a family walk, he may talk about a 'heavy' hill, or 'soggy' legs, or 'cross' thunder.[4] "Mum," wailed my nephew once, under similar circumstances, "I'm so tired, my benders are snapping." Very often, a simple question will help him to put his perceptions of sameness into words. "What does it look like? – sound like? – feel like? – taste like? – smell like?" (Record his answers then and there, if you can. You think you will remember, but you may not, and kick yourself.) Arrange what he says in lines, like poetry. It *is* poetry: all of us are poets before we are anything else.

A good way in is to talk to your child about books you are reading together. After I had broken through into reading with a much older child, by exploring Ted Hughes' *The Iron Man*, I asked him to describe the central character. "What do his eyes look like? What do his ears look like? His arms? His feet?" The replies from Lea (all the similes were his own) became a poem which I transcribed, and Lea typed and illustrated. The rest of the staff agreed that it was a superb piece of work: I was jumping up and down and showing it to everybody.

Acting as a scribe for your child is also an excellent way of helping him to read. Write down poems and stories from his dictation, and he will have no difficulty in reading them back to you. (Of course he can read them, he has just made them up himself.) For instance, Edward has severe literacy problems. His reading age at eleven was 6.1, and his written work was indecipherable, as can be seen from his attempt at a diagnostic dictation, on entry:

Diagnostic Dictation

Sept. 85

one daue' ⅌ as i wos wolt drsret
b lhy hrz zhe sounz oP zraliy
i zrnz and sou dnzmu zhe
saue dorc hor ro. a f·rzm.
'wo hows. 1⅌ shrsz ror
an apxh from ma dhr zo
gir him" i now war you
szdey. i sat. sou i rmrz
zhe danz oP my ran cowz
aod zhzlu iz a rowz
his rac eod let him dac
i onz zhe gat end
with szsrshn he gapz
in zo hic own zhelz
i wos cohz zat hewos.
saf a wau rrom zhe
hows zhnpie and danzs
zhnrie.

9

```
THE IRON MAN........by Lea, 15 yrs

The Iron Man: —
His eyes look like headlamps,
His ears look like dustbin lids,
His arms look like car axles,
His feet are like Hopper buses.
He walks along
Clanking
Grinding
Squeaking.
He eats cars
Tractors
Trucks.
He twists round barbed wire fencing
Like candy floss,
Twirls it up,
Opens his mouth wide
And plonks it in.
At night
He walks into the deep
Black
Crashing
Sea.

10th March 1986
```

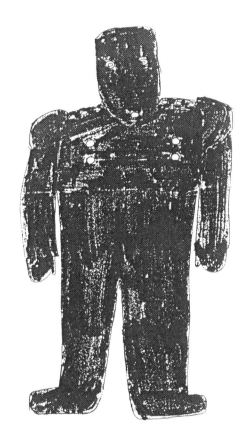

But the ideas were there in his head, and somehow I had to help him to get them out. He hugely enjoyed using a computer concept keyboard, with another teacher, which involved pressing words on an inlay sheet in front of him. These words would then appear, miraculously, in the appropriate blank spaces on the screen. By means of this process Edward had described a 'beast' as 'slimy' and 'spiky', and was quite beginning to fancy himself as an author. Later that day I suggested he should develop the story further and dictate it to me. This idea was well received, and Edward's monster took shape forthwith, in response to a few guiding questions. In spite of my faith in the unlimited potential of all children, even I was taken aback by the flood of confident and articulate language which proceeded to pour forth. I was fascinated to discover that at first, the influence of the concept keyboard vocabulary was very evident. But as Edward became increasingly absorbed in the account, his own natural words took over, portraying in a marvellous display of imagination a creature that has never existed before or since. (I was given a language lesson when he told me that during the day the monster went into his massive cave and shut his massive door, because he was nocturnal. "That means he only comes out at night, Miss," explained Edward, in case I didn't know. "Thank you, Edward," I said faintly, "I'll make a note of that.")

Here is the complete description:

Edwards's Monster

There is a spiky, slimy monster with massive talon-like claws, called Zeph. It is a little bit furry, but it isn't like your ordinary fur. It is so stiff it feels like your hair does when you wash it with soap instead of shampoo.

He is so big he looks down on the trees. He can breathe under water, so he lies in wait at the bottom of ponds. He grabs the ducks and the geese when they fly in and land on the water.

In the daytime he goes in his massive cave and shuts his massive door, and only comes out at night – he is nocturnal. He has brilliant eye sight so he can see his prey at night – foxes, cows, goats, sheep and also boats. He can sense water from over five thousand miles away. (He prefers salt water because he has ulcers.) When he gets to some water he slurps it all up through a stupendously huge straw leaving the boats high and dry, stuck in the mud, all in one pile next to the end of the straw. He scoops them up in his hand, throws them in his mouth, and they go shooting down his throat. He gets lots of splinters in his stomach, which is why he has ulcers.

Later, I had a brilliant idea. (The children have most of the brilliant ideas, but I am allowed to have some. Any primary school teacher would have thought of this straightaway, but I had to discover it for myself.) Reading back my handwritten version was difficult for Edward. So if I printed each sentence on one page, in large clear print, and Edward illustrated it, we would have a superb production of his masterpiece, which could be used for reading practice. I knew already that Edward was an artist (as well as an author) of considerable talent. To my delight, he responded enthusiastically once again. Here are some extracts from the finished work:

There is a
spiky, slimy monster
with massive
talon-like claws
called Zeph.

Zeph.

It is a little bit
furry, but it isn't
like your ordinary fur.
It is so stiff it feels
like your hair does
when you wash it
with soap instead
of shampoo.

ZEPH

As we completed each page, Edward read aloud all the pages included so far, then tallied[5] words of his own choice, with my help if he needed it. Naturally he chose the longest and most interesting words to tally – 'massive', 'shampoo, 'nocturnal', 'thousand', 'stupendous' – and looked modestly nonchalent when I enthused. Faced with tangible evidence of his own special gifts, he was beginning to think of himself as someone who could, rather than someone who couldn't.

Children of all ages seem to like monsters. Our work with Edward pointed us in the direction of another good idea. It was time for a fourth year module on 'Books, Writing and Kids', which I had initiated, as a class teacher, twelve months earlier. A score of fourth years had visited our local primary school, and shared books with the youngsters there. Now that I was concentrating on Special Education work, another teacher decided she would like to offer a similar module. Would I prepare an instruction sheet, and take the initial lesson?

I agreed, with a certain amount of dismay. Some year groups, willy nilly, carry reputations with them throughout the school. The students I had worked with were bright, enthusiastic, positive, cooperative. But the present fourth years had unfortunately made a name for themselves as hostile, rebellious and negative. I had taken one group for mainstream English when they were third years, and none of us enjoyed the experience at all. So I didn't look forward to the lead lesson. Yvette whispered when I arrived that they weren't very motivated: the idea of a 'community service' module had been greeted with sour animosity.

Maybe I had better begin by scotching that description. We weren't bothered about getting them to do 'community service', I told them. What we were concerned about were the people they were going to become when they left school, and the jobs they were going to do. For almost all of them, whatever else they did, would probably be parents within the next ten years; and whether they got good jobs, or mediocre jobs, or no jobs at all, the most important job they would ever do would be their job as parents. The purpose of this module was to find some small children for them to practise on, so they could look forward to their own parenthood with confidence, and in full awareness of just how vital they were going to be in their children's lives. I told them that parents were the best teachers of literacy, and that they could do a more effective job than any teacher ever could. (The liked that.) I told them about Glenn Doman and the brain damaged children who had learned to read fluently because of his work; about Liz Waterland and the idea of apprenticeship. I talked to them for an hour, and they listened, absorbed, in total silence. (Afterwards Yvette wailed at me, "They have *never* listened to me like that." "They never listened to *me* like that, last year," I said. "I couldn't even get them to listen for five minutes, let alone an hour. They only listened today because I was telling them about something real – about the real people they are going to be, and how important they are.")

This is the instruction sheet I gave them – you will notice how it was inspired by Edward's 'monster' story:

14

BOOKS, WRITING AND KIDS

Your main purpose is *not* to 'help with reading' – that will happen as a sort of byproduct. Your main purpose is to enjoy exploring books and making books, together with your partner.

You cannot do this without getting to know your partner, so spend as much time as you like on making friends. Remember that it's also important for your partner to get to know you – you must tell him/her quite a bit about yourself.

SESSION 1

Discussion

Here are some simple questions you can ask to get you talking. Take your partner's answers seriously, and really listen. You don't have to ask these questions if you have better ones of your own.

1. What did you do yesterday?
    Follow up: Shall I tell you something funny that happened to me yesterday?

2. Tell me about television and what you like about it.
    Follow up: My very favourite programme is . . . but my sister can't bear it.

3. Tell me about school and what you like about it.
    Follow up: You know I can still remember my very first day at school. Such and such happened.

4. Describe your house.
    Follow up: Something interesting about my house is . . .

5. What is the most amount of money you can imagine? (You may be surprised at the answer.) If you had that much money, what would you spend it on first?

Book sharing

When you feel the time is right, move on to sharing a book. Explain that you are trying to find out what kinds of books are popular with five year olds, for a survey (make your partner feel grownup and important). So can you look at a book and find out what he thinks about it?

a) To begin with, just look at the pictures together. Ask your partner to tell you about the pictures. You can ask questions like "What is he doing? Why do you think he is doing that?" Your partner may well 'tell you a story' that is quite different from the one in the book – this doesn't matter at all. You are getting him involved on an equal basis.

b) Now tell (*not* read) the 'book' story to your partner, referring to the pictures as you go along. This is not the 'correct' version – just an alternative version. Make it as interesting as you can, and encourage your partner to join in with comments.

c) Ask your partner's opinion of the book. *Listen* to what he says, and write it down. Ask questions like "Which are your favourite bits? If you were making this book, are there any more pictures you would put in it?"

By now you have probably spent enough time with the book for one session, so move on to something else. At the following session, you will return to the same book and *read* it to your partner.

Book making

Tell your partner he can probably make a book himself that is just as good, if not better. Why don't you make a book about a monster together? (You can choose another topic if you prefer.)

a) Ask your partner questions about this monster, and write down his answers:

1. What shall we call our monster?
2. How big is he?

16

3. Is he furry? What is his fur like?
4. What colour is he?
5. Does he have a tail? What is it like?
6. Where does he live?
7. What does he eat? How does he catch it?
8. What is his favourite drink?
9. When he gets ill, what is wrong with him? (Tummy aches, headaches splinters, cuts and grazes etc.)

b) Now explain you are going to make this story into a proper book. You are going to write down what your partner has just made up. He is going to be the 'illustrator' (with help).

Print, in large clear letters, your partner's first answer. Read it to your partner while you write it. This is going to be the first page in the book. You need a picture to go with it. Your partner *could* draw this – or, if not, you draw it for your partner to colour in. If you have sticky paper, your partner could 'colour' the picture with little bits of torn up sticky paper – you help if necessary.

Glue your page of writing on one side of the book, and the picture opposite. Read the page to your partner, pointing to the words, remarking on especially good bits.

Say, "Can you show me the word 'monster'?" (*Not* "What is this word?") "Can you see the word 'monster' anywhere else?" Show your partner where the word is if he cannot find it, and praise him enthusiastically. You want to make him feel clever, confident, and that he *can* read.

Carry on making pages like this until the end of the session. Have a break every now and then for a chat.

LATER SESSIONS

Discussion

Spend some time getting to know each other again.

Book sharing

Talk about the printed book again. Explain that the book can tell you the story all by itself, and you need to know what your partner thinks of this. Read the whole book to your partner, pointing to the words, as interestingly as possible. Then flip through the book, saying, "Can you find the word so and so?" (Do this with just two or three words. *Long,* interesting words are much easier to spot than little short ones!) If he can't, *you* point them out.

At this session, or later ones, you can introduce a new book, or stay with the same one if your partner really likes it. Go through a new book as you did in Session 1.

Book making

Read aloud each page you have made so far, pointing to the words as you go along. At the end of the first page, say, "Now you read it back to me. I'll help you." Point to each word, encourage your partner to say it, and help him any time he gets stuck. *Don't* 'sound out' the words – it's the meaning that's important. Praise him at the end of each page and remind him how many words he got *right.*

Carry on making pages until you have finished the 'monster' book. Write a title page in large letters, adding 'Written and illustrated by . . .' (Child's name)

Later, my phone began to ring. It was Yvette. "Let me tell you about what happened today," she would declare excitedly, and launch into yet another enthusiastic account.

Her first piece of information was about Matthew. Matthew had gone dark red with embarrassment at the very thought of going over to the primary school. He couldn't possibly help little kids to read and write – he had literacy problems himself. Unfortunately, when Matthew had been a first year, I had been the 'remedial' teacher, taking 'remedial' groups. Matthew had therefore been identified, in his own eyes and everybody else's, as a 'remedial' student. Little use now to tell him that I was doing things differently, and that the children I worked with were no longer

18

'remedial' but 'special', part of the mainstream along with the rest. Yvette, though, acted out of inspiration, refusing to entertain for a moment the idea that Matthew wasn't much needed. Would he join forces with Stuart, whose handwriting, to say the least, was pretty awful scribble? No reason why two fourth years couldn't work with one youngster. Stuart would write down the child's story, in the first instance, because after all his spelling was reasonable – and then if Matthew could print it out neatly – he did have very attractive handwriting . . . ? Matthew began to think that maybe he could. So there the three of them had sat, engrossed in the same undertaking; and who had been the master craftsmen, and who the apprentice? Yvette concluded in triumph.

The next time she phoned, it was about Lloyd, and Mark. Did I remember Lloyd and Mark? Yes indeed, they were in my English group as third years, and had not brightened my life. "Why do we have to come to school anyway?" was their general attitude then. But Lloyd – *Lloyd* – had been most put out at the prospect of missing a trip to the primary school because of a parental holiday. "Miss – don't let *anyone else* work with my partner. You won't, will you? I'll finish the book with him next time, honest!" And he did. Mark decided to share Raymond Briggs' *Father Christmas* with a partner, because he loved it himself, especially the bad language. ("There isn't any bad language, Mark." "Yes there is, Miss, it's awful, look what he's saying there: *!!!xx*'!") He struck up a friendship with a child who shared his own zany humour, and proceeded to inspire illustrations to match.

All too soon the module rushed to its end, and Yvette called me in to the top site staffroom one day when I was whisking past. "Look," she said, "look." I looked. There was a tumble of booklets, each one bound and spiralled by Yvette, each one unique, with all manner of monsters glaring from the pages. The stories painstakingly and beautifully printed by the fourth years. I forgot everything else as we gloated through them together. "I didn't get anything like this from my last year's group!" I told her. "They're super. And isn't it interesting how well the boys have done."

We knew we weren't just looking at an array of booklets to be filed away under the heading '4th year coursework'. We were contemplating, smugly, the future fathers who would be leading their own children into literacy, and undertaking the process with delight and pride. (We were no less happy about the future mothers. But fathers so often feel excluded from parenting. Here were some, we thought, who wouldn't be.)

Footnotes

2. Liz Waterland, *'Read with me* and After', *Signal* 51, September 1986.
3. See Susanne Langer, *Philosophy in a New Key*, pp. 138-142. See also pp 102-104 in this booklet.
4. Jane Boutrell, 'Out of the mouth of babes', *The Guardian*, August 12 1986.
5. See Book Two, *Saying Written Words Aloud*, Section VIII, for a detailed description of tallying.

III

Handwriting that helps

Understanding print happens first. Then saying written words aloud. No sense in teaching children to write before they have fallen in love with books, before they know the purpose of writing. But when they have seen and read their own words, written down, learning to write makes sense. If you can make these magical shapes yourself, there is no need to wait for a scribe . . .

It was my daughters who showed me that pre-school children were quite capable of learning to write, if only the materials were to hand. When Helen was four, and Gwynneth nearly three, they could both read anything they could understand. The place where many of their new words had first appeared was the wall in their bedroom, which I had turned into a blackboard by the simple expedient of painting the entire bottom half with blackboard paint. What was more natural for them than to pick up a piece of coloured chalk and trace over some of their favourite words? It dawned on me that if I wanted Helen to be able to write independently, there was little left for me to do, apart from making clear to her just what was going on. She would soon be starting school, and might as well be able to write before she got there. Gwynneth, however, became highly indignant when she saw me playing this new and exciting game with her older sister. She grabbed a piece of chalk and insisted on joining in. No, I explained, she was too little, she couldn't. Gwynneth in a fury proceeded to scream the place down until I hastily revised my opinions and assured her that she wasn't too little at all, of course she could do it.

Feeling my way, I taught them to print, because printing most closely resembles the forms of words in books. For the same reason, most primary school children begin by learning to print. They don't attempt 'joined writing' for years, and are often still happily printing when they get to secondary school.

Printing, however, has several disadvantages. It's a surprisingly difficult form of writing to do well. Lower case letters start in all kinds of different places – 'e's on the line, 'a's and 'c's in mid air, 'b's higher up still, and 'f's up and over there. It's also a staccato, halting process – the emphasis is on the formation of the separate letters, not on the flow of the word as a whole. But just when a child has attained a reasonable facilty with printed letters, he has to set to work and learn how to join the wretched things together!

Why don't we teach him 'joined writing' first? Cursive handwriting is often recommended for dyslexic children. Here it is:

HANDWRITING SHEET

⌐ rainbow   ∪ u-shaped connector

⌐ rocker   ∪ saucer connector

a b c d e f g h i j k l m
n o p q r s t u v w x y z

abcdefghijklmnopqrstuvwxyz

The quick brown fox jumps over
the lazy dog.

A B C D E F G H I J K
L M N O P Q R S T U
V W X Y Z

22

Cursive writing may not be as immediately attractive as italic script, say, but it's a more helpful form of writing for a dyslexic child to learn. Dyslexic printing is often laboured and chaotic, dotted haphazardly with capital letters even in the middle of words, because of the visualizing problem. The child cannot see in his mind's eye the way the letters are supposed to look, so much of his writing is sheer guesswork.

If one of a child's senses is letting him down, not to be relied on, then we must help him to learn by means of one of the others. When we're writing, as well as the sense of sight, we also use the sense of 'feel'. Even with our eyes shut we can write legibly, because our fingers have learned to form the shapes of words without reference to what our eyes can see.

The point about cursive writing is that it is easily learned 'by the feel'. Evey lower case letter begins with either a 'rainbow' or a 'rocker', and it always begins on the line. Another feature is that words are written as wholes, without once lifting the pencil from the paper; so that gradually the feeling, the meaning and the spelling of a word are all stored in the child's fingertips, which is where learning to write happens anyway. There are only two basic 'connectors' – a thin u-shaped connector, used when joining from the bottom of a letter, and a 'saucer' connector, for joining from the tops of letters (*ꝏ*, *ꞃ*, *ᴠ* and *ᴡ*). These connectors are sometimes modified, but the basic ideas are constant, and can be readily discussed.

Once we abandon the idea that learning to form letters helps with learning to read (it doesn't), and realize that writing can and should be deferred until a child is at home with books, it begins to dawn that we don't have to start with printing. The first words a child writes do not need to look exactly like the ones in books: he is so familiar with their shapes by now, he can easily appreciate the slight modification in their appearance that happens when the letters are linked together.

If you are teaching a pre-schooler to write, as I taught Helen and Gwynneth, wait until he is clearly trying to trace over the shapes of words on his blackboard. Suppose he is investigating the printed word 'ghost'. Explain that words are much easier to write if the letters are joined, and write the same word, in cursive writing, alongside the printed version: '*ghost*'. "Look, isn't this crafty – you can write the whole word without once taking the chalk away. We begin the '*g*' with a rainbow – we call it that because it looks like one – and then a rocker joins on the '*h*' – do you see?

You have a go over the top of my word – I'll help you if you get in a muddle. From then on, write all his words on the blackboard in cursive writing, and make lots of paper and thick felt tips available so that he can practise his new skill with these materials too.

Help him to trace over, perhaps, one word a day. Talk about the shapes of the letters and their connectors, in detail, both when you are writing the word, and again when he is going over it. This will help him to remember the appropriate feelings.

For example, here is how you could talk about ' *pond* ':

"Start with a short rocker – then straight down, a long stick. Backtrack up again, and right round until you're touching your long stick. That's the 'p' done. Swing round and up, on to your 'o' – but stop at the very top, in the middle, and backtrack right round to the middle again. Now, you join from the 'o' at the top, with a saucer connector – curl down and up, that's right. We're starting the 'n' now, straight down, backtrack up, start coming away when you're nearly at the top of the straight stick, but carry on upwards, so your arch is nice and curved, the same height as the stick. Well done – come on down, and now you want a thin u-shaped connector to take you up on to your 'd'. Round you go on the 'd', dip down a bit at the side, backtrack, right round and straight up. Come straight down again, and finish him off with a very small tail. Well done – that's splendiferious – I'm so proud of you!"

When your child writes on paper, it should slant up towards the right for a righthanded child, and up to the left if he is left handed (see illustration, taken from S.T. Orton's book, *Reading, Writing and Speech Problems in Children*, Chapman and Hall). This enables a child to move his hand easily across the page without smudging what he has just written.

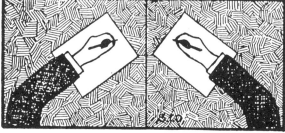

A sketch to show the corresponding positions of the paper and hand for left- and right-handed writers.

24

Of course he can learn printing too, but later, when the words he wants to write are already coming easily and fluently from his pen. He can alter the cursive style to suit his own personality, or experiment with the italic script if that appeals. But because he has learned cursive writing first, you have given him a solid foundation on which to build, and also the confidence that writing is nothing to worry about, something he can easily do. More children than we suppose are at least mildly dyslexic, and if all our children become proficient with cursive handwriting from the beginning, then any dyslexic child will be getting the best possible start, often before his problems are even suspected. In many ways, it makes sense to teach all children 'as if they were dyslexic'. 'Normal' children will not lose out thereby, and the dyslexic will most assuredly benefit!

In Section V, I'll suggest a way of introducing cursive writing with older children.

IV

Dots, dashes and tadpoles

In other words, punctuation . . .

Once again, help your child to punctuate by apparently beginning somewhere else. The best way of doing it is not with a formal lesson on 'the use of the full stop'! You don't begin when he's writing at all. You begin when you're reading to him; but when you can feel his own desire to write gathering force, and trembling in the wings.

"Look," you can say, when you've finished the bedtime story, "have you noticed the funny little marks that sometimes come between the words? They're like the stops and pauses we use when we're talking. But writers would get fed up putting 'stop', and 'pause', or 'make your voice ask a question', all the time. So they use these marks instead, which are much quicker. Look, that dot means the end of a whole idea. And the new idea begins with a capital letter, to remind you. Can you see? A whole idea like that is called a sentence. It begins with a capital letter and ends with a full stop.

"Sometimes you want to have a breath very quickly, in the middle of a sentence, before you've got to the end. So writers put a little tadpole shape, to tell you when to do that. It's called a comma. You don't breathe for as long as you do at a full stop, and the meaning of the sentence keeps on going. Can you find any more commas?

"This is a very clever sign – it tells your voice to ask a question. So we call it a question mark, and just bung it in at the end of every question. And this is an exclamation mark – it means you've got to say the sentence in a pop eyed sort of way!

"You would get very bogged down if the whole page was just covered with one big wodge of print, wouldn't you. It would be quite uncomfortable to read. So writers divide up their stories into nice short blocks, called paragraphs. Each paragraph starts away from the edge, look, as a signal, and when you get to the end, the rest of the line is left empty. You can have lots of sentences in one paragraph, but all the sentences are talking about the same thing. It's a bit like something on television As long as the camera is looking at one scene, the sentences go together in one paragraph. When the scene changes, you start a new paragraph. Simple!

"These signs are called speech marks, you use them when somebody is talking. You know in comics, words coming out of the characters' mouths are put inside bubbles, to show you who's saying what – well, speech marks do the same job when you just have print, no pictures. They're like bubbles – they go round the outside edges of what is being said."

Of course you don't plough through all these explanations at the same time, but bit by bit, arouse your child's interest in punctuation marks, and the jobs they do, until he is noticing them for himself. Then, later, when he is writing, you can remind him to use the appropriate signs. "I expect you'll want to make that into a sentence, won't you, so don't forget to start with a capital letter, and finish off with a full stop . . . Write a story with people talking, then you can use proper speech marks – that'll be fun. Start a new paragraph whenever a different person is going to start speaking, just like in your books . . ."

And your child will find himself punctuating what he writes, fom the beginning, easily and naturally, without having to worry about it.

V

The problem of spelling

When Helen and Gwynneth realized they could generate written words themselves, their writing exploded all over the house. Since they had first learned to write on a wall, walls were naturally places to write. Books too. Other people had written in books, that meant so could they. Although part of me was rather intrigued by the idea of a home bedecked in scribble, I realized we had to have some guidelines. Like Henry Ford, I decreed they could write on any wall they wanted, so long as it was black. They could write in *Ladybird* books, because they were cheap and expendable, but not in any others. And I would give them all the paper and exercise books they wanted. By and large, they kept these rules pretty well, although the occasional word did sneak its way onto the living room walls, greeting us cheerily when we sat down for breakfast. Many a page in a *Ladybird* book was faithfully copied, in its entirety, and in this way, my daughters more or less taught themselves to write. Soon mere copying was not enough, and blank lined paper came into its own. I still treasure many of the thin exercise books we used, crammed with their own written words, and decorated with titles from the mysterious world of childhood they inhabited: 'The Cloud Prince', 'The Adventure of the Rumbajoo'.

If writing follows in its proper place, emerging when the time is ripe from a child's love of books, and his confident ability to match written words with speech, he should hardly have to worry about the mechanics of writing. There is no virtue in allowing him to write with not a full stop to be seen, capital letters in all the wrong places, and spelling that is wild and wonderful. A child learns nothing from making mistakes except how to go on making them. But when he is soaked in written words before ever he sets pen to paper, then punctuation, paragraphing, spelling will usually come of themselves.

Gwynneth, at three, stumped for a spelling, would call out, "Mum, I want to write 'garage'." (Heaven only knows why.) "Make the word say 'gu'.

Now make it say 'gă', what letter do you think? Good, an 'ă', that's right. You want a 'ru' to make it say 'găr'. Now make it say 'gara', you want another . . .? Well done, another 'ă'. Now you want a 'gu'. Now the word says 'garag', so you need a magic 'ĕ' to make the 'gu' into a 'ju'." "I've done it, Mum! I've written 'garage'! Come and see!"

Obviously I couldn't expect her to look up words in a dictionary, but this approach seemed more instinctive than just telling her the right letters. I called it 'talking her through a word'. Years later, it dawned on me that it was the mirror image of a process already mastered: what I had dubbed 'phonic translation', but in reverse. Because fitting sounds to letters was such a familiar procedure for Gwynneth, she had no problem now in fitting letters to sounds.

Neither Helen nor Gwynneth had any difficulty with spelling as they grew older. The words for whatever they wanted to write came to hand, and the spellings came too, very soon without any need for Mum's intervention. It had all been so easy, I just assumed that accurate spelling followed on automatically from abundant exposure to books.

It doesn't. Not until I was working with older children, in secondary education, did I realize that a youngster could be an avid reader, and still find that spelling was a chancy business. The same word might appear in any number of ways, sometimes all on one page. 'Apple', 'alepp', 'plead', 'pelap', 'abble' . . . After a long period of sheer bafflement, I tracked down the only explanation that made sense. Children with spelling difficulties were having trouble because they couldn't visualize words accurately.[6]

It isn't, in fact, a problem of memory, although the experts often tell us it is, assuming that explains everything. But a child with a visualizing peculiarity can remember the spellings of words all right. It's just that he can remember them too well – far too many of them for one word! He has a problem, not of memory, but of choice: how to decide which of the many equivalent forms of the word in his head is the correct version?

I know now that my first task, when tackling spelling with a youngster, can be to point out to him that the spellings of most words are constant; and that writing the same word in five different ways is going to land him in trouble. Often this is a strange idea. It hasn't occurred to him that his spelling isn't perfectly acceptable! (I try to proceed with tact, and sympathetic noises of regret for the many delicious spellings which will have to be rejected. They are, after all, familiar friends.)

Sometimes, though, the child has already realized that spelling words 'the way they look' doesn't seem to answer. Not only do other people find it hard to understand what he has written; occasionally he cannot even read it himself. So, exasperated, he abandons the visual strategy, and plumps instead for spelling words 'the way they sound'. He knows that several words might still be incorrect, but at least his writing is legible.

In order to appreciate what is happening, where the blockages are likely to be, and the best ways of helping children around them, it may be a good idea to establish a general theory of spelling at this point.

We can begin by asking a simple question. It is so simple that the answer is abundantly obvious, which is why we don't ask it very often. But it holds the key to the entire complex jungle of literacy skills.

Instead of asking, 'How do children learn – to understand print, to read aloud, to write and to spell?' let's go to the other end of this language learning activity, and ask ourselves instead, 'What are words made of? – What are spoken words made of? What are written words made of?'

The answers are somewhat surprising. We use more things to make words with than we consciously suppose. Spoken words, of course, are made of sounds: but there are two different ways of experiencing sounds. We can hear them, or we can utter them. So a spoken word can be a pattern of heard sounds, or a pattern of vocal sensations (or both at once).

The tired answer to the question 'What are written words made of?' Is that written words are made of letters. (Can we stop asking these silly questions and get on to something useful?)

Thousands of years of history not withstanding, written words are not made of letters . . .

The reason that the idea of 'letters' is unhelpful and misleading, is that when we think of a 'letter', we think of something that has a name, and a sound value. The name of this shape: 'b' is 'bee', and its sound value is 'bu'.

Written words are not made of letters, they are made of shapes.

Of course they are made of shapes. This is why deaf people can read them even if they have no idea of the 'sound values' of any of the letters.

They don't have to. The meanings of the words are inherent in the shapes, and the deaf reader looks through the words to perceive the meanings.

Thinking of shapes rather than letters liberates the imagination. A word can be just a pattern of shapes, and it can represent meaning directly, with no necessary reference to any other kind of pattern. But there are all sorts of ways of experiencing shapes. You can see them, you can feel them (which is why blind people can read), you can describe them in the air with your hand. If you are holding a pencil while you do this, the pencil reproduces on paper the shapes your hand is feeling, and these patterns of shapes become in their turn words perceptible to sight, long after your hand has moved away.

What it boils down to is that there are four different kinds of words in everyday use. Spoken words are 'heard' words or 'uttered' words. Written words can be thought of as 'seen' words or 'handwriting movement' words.

When I'm giving talks about this, I usually have an apple which represents the meaning of a word. The different word forms are raisins on the end of cocktail sticks, stuck into the apple. It's not an exact analogy, because raisins are blobs rather than patterns, but it loosens the thinking. Here it is in diagrammatic form:

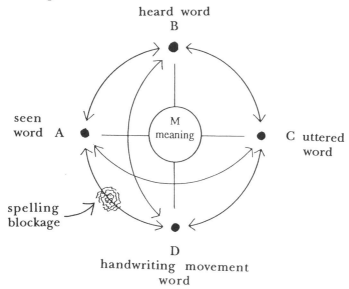

31

The point is that any kind of pattern, perceptible to any one of the senses, can function as a word in its own right. It can represent meaning directly. This is when language is transparent: we go straight through the patterns to the meanings. We can see the meaning of a word; we can hear it; we can feel it in our mouth and voice as we utter it; or we can feel it with our hand as we write it. The meanings are as immediate and palpable as the patterns themselves.

A language symbol doesn't have to be a pattern, theoretically, a blob would do. But in practice patterns are essential because only patterns can be endlessly differentiated from each other. Language is bursting with a multitude of words, so it has to have a mutitude of patterns to keep up. It's helpful to think of each pattern as a series: of sounds, or vocal sensations, or shapes, or handwriting movements.

Because you can have four different forms of a word, all meaning the same thing, the different words are equivalent. No one form is *the* word, or some how more absolute than its fellows. The constantly shifting, infinitely possible meaning, is the absolute. As far as the words to represent it are concerned, any one of the raisins can come first.

It follows that any raisin can be independently matched with any other raisin (see diagram). The differing pattern sequences all align with each other. A series of heard sounds can be matched with a series of uttered sounds, *or* with a series of shapes, *or* with a series of handwriting movements.

This is an analytical, translating procedure, and the way you operate on words to match them is totally different from the way you perceive their meanings. Now you have to divide a word up into its component parts, so you can tally each piece with a corresponding piece from an equivalent form. Then as soon as you have obtained an equivalent form, that word too gives you direct access to the same meaning.

It's quite beautiful, really.

Heard words or seen words, though, are usually the first kinds of words experienced by a child. He has to invest what he hears or sees with meaning, before he generates meaningful words himself. But once they have become an integral part of his life, he can think about translating them. Words he hears can be matched with vocal sensations as he discovers how to say them. Or by moving a pencil across the page, he can translate the words he reads into words he himself creates. We could divide the different word forms into 'expressive' words (generated by the child) and 'impressive' (?) forms – the ones he first learns to understand. A translating process – from an 'impressive' form to an 'expressive' one – is almost invariably used when words are generated.

The difficulty for dyslexic children seems to be that they cannot learn to spell by visualizing words. When they try to spell words by translating the way they look, their inner perception lets them down. What they write is indeed a faithful translation of what they 'see', but what they 'see' can change its form so many times that their initial attempts at independent spelling are bizarre. The direct translating route between A and D is blocked.

The way to crack this puzzle is to recognize that if one translating network is blocked, *there is always an alternative route.* You can spell a word by visualizing the way it looks, and match that image with the equivalent movements of your pencil (A to D). Or, you can think of the sequence of sounds in a word, and translate that into the same series of pencil movements (B to D). Or you can translate the series of sounds into a series of vocal sensations first, and then arrive at the same matching series of handwriting movements (B + C to D). (We all know children who need to say the words aloud while they write them.) Very often, of course, we do all three. We think of the way the word looks, and how it sounds, and how it feels when we say it, at the same time as we're writing it.

Dyslexic children cannot rely on their inner perception of written words: so they have to shift to a different reference point. Spoken words are, on the whole, reliable, and seem to keep their forms to a much greater extent than written words do. (You can establish this for yourself just by talking to a child. He may get some of his spoken words in a muddle, but in general his pronunciations are likely to be accurate.) The royal road to spelling, then, for a dyslexic child, means that he has to abandon all temptation to spell words 'the way they look', and concentrate instead on translating 'the way they sound'.

Some children seem to manage this more easily than others. I've already indicated that some may well hit on the strategy by themselves. But many don't, and we need to be aware of this, so we can make it available to all children.

It's a specific skill, which has virtually nothing to do with reading. The best way to approach it is to think of it more as a mathematical game. The child is learning to operate on sets of sounds and sets of shapes. First he adds on the sounds until he arrives at a complete set (a whole spoken word). Next he divides the set up into bits again, so he can tally each bit with a corresponding shape. Then he adds up both sets (sounds and shapes) at the same time. He finishes with two complete and corresponding sets. He can think of them together, or separately; the set of shapes he has generated can go its own way if it wants to, with direct and independent access to the meaning.

Let's clothe the process in its more familiar form. Here is a child learning to tally the word 'pond', so as to spell it. First, he adds on the sounds as he goes along, saying 'pu, pŏ, pon, pond'. Next, he builds up the sounds again, but this time he visualizes a 'p' shape when he says 'pu', and writes it down. He says 'pŏ', and adds on an 'o', 'pon' and writes the 'n', 'pond' and finishes with a 'd'. The written word is now complete, and can mean 'a small expanse of water' all by itself.

This procedure is very handy for a dyslexic child. Even if the word 'pond' is arranging itself as 'pnod' in his head, he can use the spoken word to straighten it out again, and make it behave. He can not only spell the word correctly – he *knows* he can spell it correctly, because he can check it by tallying it against the spoken form. Which is very morale boosting.

If you have already shown a child how to tally regular words while he reads them, you can easily show him how to tally back again, from sounds to shapes. I do this by just asking a child to 'tally' a word out loud: 'hu, hĕ, hel, help'. Then he has to tally the word in his head, while he spells the word orally. Finally I ask him to write the word, again tallying it, out loud or silently, as he goes along.

In fact most children find this a handy way to spell. We all tend to mutter words to ourselves while we're writing: so being able to tally shapes with sounds, in detail, gives us an additional way of 'checking our sums'! When we're helping young children with the beginnings of writing, we often demonstrate the procedure instinctively, as I did for Helen and Gwynneth.

It's because it has such a useful part to play in this respect that keep coming back to phonics. Those old fashioned phonic reading primers may have murdered the love of reading for generations of children, but they did do something, and teachers knew it. They tackled the spelling problem, and they tackled it effectively. Children who got a toe hold on written words by means of phonics could sometimes lever themselves up, and slowly and painfully find their own way into the world of books. Because they were already accustomed to 'tallying' written words, they carried on tallying them while they read, and so found they could spell without too much trouble.

Naturally we don't reintroduce phonic reading books all over the place! All we have to do is to recognize that 'phonic translation' is a separate and useful skill in its own right. Children don't need phonics 'for' reading, because they can learn to read far more joyously without it. But they do need to practise phonics 'with' reading. They need to be able to tally letters and sounds, while they're reading, almost without noticing; so that when they come to write, the letters they need will just pop into their heads.

This is where my work with Edward is illuminating. Edward, you will remember, has learned to read brilliantly, by absorbing whole books in pretty much the way that a deaf person reads. (See Book One). He doesn't tally words at all, while he's reading, he sees their meanings directly.

There is a snag. Edward has got so good at this that he still can't spell for toffee! The words he visualizes are jumbling themselves up as they always did, but his natural inclination is to carry on spelling them 'the way they look'. Here is his attempt at a dictation exercise, halfway through his third year (aged 13), when his independent reading was already well under way: (See following page)

You can see what is happening. Because Edward doesn't tally written words with spoken words while he reads, it hasn't occurred to him that he can tally them back from spoken words, when he writes. So I have to teach him to do this.

It isn't enough, incidentally, just to teach Edward 'phonics for spelling'. He has to be able to translate words in both directions, so that he can check what he has written, and make sure it is correct. Somehow, he has to learn to tally words while he's reading, as well as writing.

Lawt one nub my
Brand Woak me Saing,?
"Weub uow inoue a braran
in my noaw he a it can -
baF,"
I uad Skalieuc
Scraul in to my trouksar
buree we uar away. The
luts of the Siule glouk
dbneuth, the Stars abuf.
I wauus bging to wunlr abal
are badncusn wan I kauk
Sulu of the Sping nuP agu
and the Scuriss of wgt
mutruben a tupe of Fuing
Sausar wishing rauw auss. We
bauu skilille to alauo
and und essuon. to uru
ruth eP the spaltrak rugb
hauk and we saysh bauk
to a eruth and the kuull
dabek is ubraur aulk e luFt

See Margaret Peters, *A Diagnostic and Remedial Spelling Manual* (Heinemann Educational), p.21, for the original version.

When I was at my wit's end about the best way of achieving this, a child at school thrust a package into my hand, and dashed off, leaving me mystified. It was from a former colleague whose son was dyslexic, and it was a copy of our old friend *Alpha to Omega*, by Bevé Hornsby and Frula Shear. If you haven't yet come across it, the best way of describing it is probably as all the phonic reading primers rolled into one. It's called 'The A – Z of Teaching Reading, Writing and Spelling', and the two authors have specialized in teaching dyslexics. Basically it's a highly structured course, working its way from simple sentences to much more complex ones, all phonically based, and by the time a child has completed it, he can spell words like 'appropriate', 'thorough' and 'Parliament' with no trouble at all.

At first I was quite cross. "What on earth has she sent me this for?" I said to myself. "Doesn't she know I can't stand this kind of book, with no soul and no imagination, just masses of boring drill – the very worst way of teaching literacy imaginable? Yuk!" and I stuffed it to the bottom of my bag.

I have great respect for parents, though, and later that evening I dug it out again and started going through it. It gradually dawned on me that the only thing wrong with it was its title. Think of it as a 'reading' course, and it's the kiss of death. But it was exactly what Edward needed if we were going to crack the spelling. It wouldn't teach him phonics 'for' reading. But if anything could teach him phonics 'with' reading, this was the book. I simply had to apply my own philosophy to it. It would indeed give Edward masses of practice in tallying words, as a separate and quite satisfying mathematical skill. There was no need at all to suppose that he couldn't be reading *The Lord of the Rings* with full enjoyment, while he was learning to write sentences like 'The pan is hot . . . '

So I took the book with me on my next visit to Edward, and showed him how it worked. I showed him the three spelling tests, and the sorts of words he would be able to spell independently by the time he'd finished it. He riffled the pages, getting the feel of it. "Do you know what I'd like to do with this book, Miss?" he said at last. "I'd like to go all the way through it *and not leave anything out*." "Right Edward," I said, 'you're on. That's exactly what we'll do."

Our first attempts were quite funny. I adopted the apprenticeship approach of leading Edward into the book. That is, I wanted to give him the experience of doing the exercises and getting them right, and allow him little chance, to begin with, of making mistakes. It was the experience that mattered, not his 'performance'. So we reviewed all the letter sounds, at the front of the book, and I showed him how to consult the list, and work them out for himself, from the pictures, if he forgot. Then we plunged into the first set of exercises. Edward tallied his way through the word list, and we moved on to the sentences. He read all the sentences aloud. I reminded him to tally the words, and he read them slowly and hesitantly, making some mistakes, but correcting them with help.

Then I dictated each sentence back to him, word by word. He spelt a word orally to begin with (no problem there). I wrote it down in cursive handwriting, so he could observe the joins, and he looked away and wrote it 'out of his head'. When he'd finished the sentence, he read it back to me.

But something had happened in the meantime. Edward had forgotten he was supposed to be tallying the words. Since he'd written them himself, they ought to make sense, and when he read the sentences back, *he couldn't do it*. Well, he could, but he was looking for what would fit the meaning, rather than the letters. Even though he'd just written 'The dog can beg,' tallying it the while, it became 'The dog can bark' when he read it back.

I had to giggle. "Look, Edward," I said, "you can't read these sentences the way you read *The Hobbit*. If you just read them for meaning, you won't get them right when you read them aloud, because most of themd are jolly silly and don't make much sense anyway. By all means read the sentence for meaning first, silently.But then slow down, look at each word, and tally it in your head before you say it. Have another go."

Now Edward knew just what was required. There was an appreciable pause as his eyes moved along the sentence, absorbing the meaning of the whole arrangement of words.

You could almost feel the change of gear, then, as he went back to the beginning, and shifted into a different way of operating on print, the tallying mode. This time he read the sentence aloud correctly, at a slow but steady pace.

Edward makes it abundantly clear to me how different the two ways of looking at written words actually are. They are different for all of us, but most of us merge them quite early on. We see the meaning, and mentally fit sounds to the letters at the same time, without really thinking about it. Edward has to shift completely from one mode to the other, in order to operate either process. Eventually, I hope, he will be able to merge them to a much greater extent than he does now, and I encourage this:

"Right Edward, this is going to crack the spelling, isn't it? We can feel how it's working. But you need to practise it as much as you can – like swimming, or playing tennis. Every time you do some reading, go back when you've finished and read just a couple of paragraphs aloud to yourself, tallying every single word. If you do that, you'll gradually find you can spell them, much more easily. And, it'll help with the difficult words as well, when you're reading. It's another way of finding out what they mean. If you're stuck on a word, slow down and tally it – then you can always shift back into the reading mode, can't you?"

Not surprisingly, he gets fed up with *Alpha to Omega* sometimes. He would far rather spend the whole time reading his beloved books. I bribe him shamelessly. "We'll do a *bit* of spelling, then we'll spend all the rest of the time reading, I promise." It's an uphill slog, because I should have started it with him years ago. I kept thinking he could do it 'incidentally', as my other students seem able to. But as far as I can tell, Edward is more severely dyslexic than anyone else I have worked with, and he needs the consciously structured underpinnings for spelling, that happen for most of us unconsciously, while we read.

Tallying written words with spoken words is not just one route to spelling for Edward, it's his only route. This is why it is so important. When he has had ample experience of doing it with regular words, he will be able to work out how to 're-pronounce' irregular words. (See following section.) He will change the way he says them, so he can spell those words as well, by tallying back from sounds to shapes. Every word in his spelling vocabulary will tally exactly. He will know, then, that he has a means of remembering the spelling of any possible word.

The strength of *Alpha to Omega* is that the sentences *are* so lunatic! They are effective precisely because they deprive Edward of 'meaning' clues to a great extent, and he has to use his tallying. They are like an eye patch, put over a child's good eye, to make him use the lazy one. Most children learn to read aloud as a byproduct of reading for meaning (rather than the other way around, it should be noted!) And, in fact, reading aloud *is* phonics, because it involves tallying sets of shapes with sets of sounds. The more a child does this, the more he can tally shapes with sounds in ever finer and finer detail – so he ends up teaching himself a great deal about individual letter – phoneme correspondences.

Edward doesn't refer to inner speech while he's reading, so he isn't teaching himself to read aloud, so he isn't teaching himself phonics. This is why I have to ensure that he learns 'phonic translation' in a 'systematic, sequential, cumulative' way, leaving nothing out. It's the children who make least use of phonics, while they're reading, to whom it must be specifically taught.

If Edward and I keep in mind that it's a kind of mathematical game, but quite fun because we're manipulating letters rather than numbers, it isn't too bad. And all the time, his self esteem is growing because he is appropriating more and more spelling territory.

As soon as he was through the initial stages, he was able to do the exercises on his own. He had to read the sentences aloud to himself, and write them word by word without looking, checking his own sentence against the original when it was completed. Gradually he moved on to writing whole sentences from memory. At last we felt we were really on the way.

Here is a page of his work from *Alpha to Omega*. It's interesting to compare it with his dictation exercise of six months earlier.

P 22

21.9.88 Is it empty?
Can Sam go with us?
Is Len at his desk?

30.9.88 My pen is in my bag.
Bob and Ben can get it.

6.10.88 Sam left it on the desk.
Ben can get a pen from that shop.

11.10.88

p 27 1 Drop that crab, it bit me.
2 Alf has left his tin box in the loft.
3 It is such a fag to go to the shops when it is so hot.
4 I must rest, and go when it is not so hot.
5 The fish went flip flop on the slab.
6 I am glad I went on that trip to the U.S.A.

21.10.88 7 I am in such a rush to get to the flat.
8 Mum has got the ham and the plum flan, and Dad has got the grog, so we can have fun.

What does this indicate for our approach to spelling at primary level? A pet idea of mine, you may have noticed, is that instead of attempting to identify dyslexia at the earliest possible moment (which is difficult), we should instead teach all children 'as if they were dyslexic'. Until they've proved they're not! This seems to me an idea that is beautiful in its simplicity, and very easy to do. The apprenticeship approach makes it all possible. You just support every child, in every area of literacy, until he has reached independence. You don't have to worry about deciding when that point is reached. The child knows when, and he will let you know.

The earlier we start teaching phonics, to all children, as an entirely separate way of operating on print, the more fun it can be, and the less we may need to resort to a formal, structured course. (We shouldn't concern ourselves with doubts about whether or not a child has the intellectual ability to do it. It's the same sort of translating procedure he used when he was teaching himself to speak – that is, to translate heard words into uttered words.) All children need the experience of being able to read aloud accurately, because this is going to help with spelling. A child's spelling may take off by itself. But if he gets to eight or nine, say, and his spelling is still wild and wonderful, then a blitz with *Alpha to Omega*, or a similar course, is probably indicated.

So long as we never forget that what he reads, and what he makes with the words he spells 'by himself' – is something else.

41

VI

The 'sneak' collection

"So far so good," I said to Troy one morning. "We're going to forget about spelling words the way they look, because we can't rely on getting them right that way. We're concentrating on spelling them the way they sound, instead. But there's a snag."

Troy, veteran of many a spelling battle, agreed resignedly. "Yes Miss – not all words *are* spelt the way they sound. Some of them have silent letters and things."

"Well," I fished, "if the words that match sounds exactly are called regular words, what do you think we should call the other ones – the ones that don't?"

I was hoping he would come up with 'irregular', but Troy looked at me with indignation written all over his small face, and declared venomously, "I'm going to call them *sneaks*!"

So sneaks they became, for ever after.

We are so used to stumbling over the 'sneaks', we may not realize that a surprisingly high proportion of words in the English language are quite inoffensive little things, regular as clockwork. The *Alpha to Omega* programme marshals them in order battalions. Once a child is well into the programme, and his spelling is firmly re-routed by way of spoken words, he has the means of spelling confidently most of the time.

There remains the quesion of what to do about the sneaks. Because spelling words as they sound is a natural procedure for most of us, not just dyslexics, there is nearly always someone bewailing the complexities of English spelling, and agitating for its reform. We have to 'rationalize' our spelling system, say the theorists, we must oblige every last written word to arrange itself obediently alongside its spoken equivalent. Hence the i.t.a. and numerous other well meaning attempts to bring the whole thing into line.

It sounds like a sensible suggestion, until we try to decide which form of spoken language is going to be our standard. Yorkshire? The Devon dialect? Cockney? Or 'received pronunciation', which is used by only a small percentage of our children anyway? Not quite as straightforward as it seemed, this idea of spelling 'reform'.

If changing the spelling of words isn't going to work, the only alternative is to change the way they sound . . . Well, that's a non-starter – even more ludicrous than tinkering about with the spelling system. Think how daft words would sound if we started saying them the way they are spelt!

Just a moment. Don't we all do this, to some extent? When you're writing 'Wednesday', I imagine you still mutter 'Wed-nes-day' to yourself, just as you did as a child. Or 'Feb-ru-ary', 'par-li-a-ment', 'temper-a-ture'. It doesn't occur to you to *say* 'Wed-nes-day' when you're talking to someone. The two forms of the spoken word co-exist quite happily inside your head: one for talking, one for writing.

If you can do it with three or four words, why shouldn't you be able to do it with hundreds? The human mind can store an infinitely large spoken vocabulary, an infinitely large reading vocabulary. Why not a third vocabulary, parallel to the first two? A 'saying-for-spelling' vocabulary, which all children compile if they find it helpful, so that any dyslexics will thereby have the means of *choosing the right spelling.*

Colin, at eleven, burst into tears one day. "I'll *never* be able to spell 'decision', never never never." The tears dripped off his nose as he contemplated the hopelessness of his puny attempts to cope with the might of the English language, arraigned against him.

"D'you want to bet, Colin?" I said. "Look – we'll divide it into bits, like this: de-ci-si-on. Now, all we have to do is 're-pronounce' each bit, and we've turned 'decision' into a regular word! Dee-ki-si-on. You have a go."

Colin stopped sniffing and stared doubtfully at the word in front of him. "Why won't I spell it with a 'k' if I say it like that?" "Well of course you won't, because you're very sensible, and you know 'k' can never go with an 's' sound, don't you? Say the whole word again, to remind yourself, if you're in any doubt. 'Decision'. See – you just need to choose between 'c' and 's'. Try it, if you don't believe me."

Grudgingly, Colin obliged. "Dee-ki-si-on." "Very good – once more, and then from memory. "Dee-ki-si-on, dee-ki-si-on." "Now, each bit just happens to have only two letters. Spell the 'dee' bit." "D, e." "Now 'ki'."

"C, i." "And 'si'." "S, i." "Last bit, 'on' – there you are, you see, you've got it. Hold each bit in your head now, concentrate on one bit at a time, take breaths in the gaps between the bits – and spell the whole word." A prickle of electricity came from nowhere. "D, e," breath, "c, i," breath, "s, i," breath, "o, n." "And again." "D, e; c, i; s, i; o, n." Somewhere in the background someone was singing about Hertford, Hereford and Hampshire, and soggy plains in Spain; the room was full of silent music. "And *again*, Colin!" "D, e, c, i, s, i, o, n! D, e, c, i, s, i, o, n! Dee-ki-si-on! I've got it!"

"Of course you've got it – and I'll tell you something else. You've not only got it for now, but when I ask you to spell 'decision' tomorrow, you'll get it right then – and two weeks from now – and next month, and next year. You will be able to spell 'decision' for the rest of your *life*, if you just remember 'dee-ki-si-on' whenever you need to write it."

Two years later, at the beginning of a follow up session with Colin and his mum, Colin stopped me before I could say anything. "Listen Miss – dee-ki-si-on – d, e; c, i; s, i; o, n." And then a huge grin split his face in two as he remembered the exact moment when he zapped the spelling Goliath with a single stone from his sling; and realized that if he could do it with one word, he could do it with the whole bloody lot.

This is why it is important to identify the problem as one of choice, and not of memory. If we think the child's memory is letting him down, we may decide to strengthen it by giving him extensive practice with the 'Kim game', for instance. It certainly wouldn't occur to us to expect him to memorize hundreds of different forms of words, in addition to the ones he is already struggling with, and assume that he will find this helpful!

He can memorize them, and he does find it helpful. I call them 'memory boosters', and they work like a charm. 'Bee-cay-use' for 'because', 'pee-op-ul' for 'people' (or 'pee-op-lee' if the 'le' letter pattern is still unfamiliar – you vary the memory booster to suit the child). 'Ee-nor-mō-us','ex-tinc-tī-on': the vast majority of sneaks fall into place with hardly an attempt at rebellion. The child knows he can spell them because he has turned them into regular words in his head, before his pencil even approaches the paper.

Here are some more examples: 'wăl-king', 'brid-ge', 'sō-und', 'trot-ting' (so the double letter won't go missing), 'sā-id', 'sō-mē', 'lăt-e', 'fri'end', 'wŏk-ē', 'scram'bled', 'begin'ning', 'des-tin-ā-tī-on', 'pē-cū-lī-ar', 'ap-prōach-ing'.

Surprisingly few sneaks don't respond very well to simple re-pronunciation. They are the ones with awkward letter patterns like 'ough', 'ould', 'igh', 'augh'. Saying 'co-ug-hu' is more trouble than it's worth, so for these letter patterns, we use mnemonics instead.

Most of us, we discover, have a useful supply of old uncles, recently made redundant, and wondering what to do with their spare time. Some mooch around slurping gallons of beer, and put on a lot of weight in the process: 'old uncles get heavy'. (One third year scornfully rejected the beer swilling uncle, however. His uncle wasn't fat, but he did feel the cold. So the mnemonic for 'ough' had to be 'old uncles get *hypothermia*' . . .)

Other uncles, with a bit more go about them, blow their entire redundancy money on Lamborghinis or Ferraris, and blast down the M1, Toad fashion: 'old uncles like driving'.

India is near the equator (I point out on the globe I keep handy), which means that 'indians get hot'; and we resort to mythology for 'augh': 'all unicorns grow horns'. A memory booster for 'straight' thus becomes 'stra-indians get hot-t'; 'daughter' would be 'd-all unicorns grow horns-ter'. They may sound complicated to you, but try them out. Children who are determined to win the spelling war can remember them with ease, and gradually learn to park all the 'ough' words in the rocking chair along with their old uncles.

That's really all you need to cover such sneakiest of sneaks. Mnemonics occasionally come in handy for whole words: 'big elephants can't always use small entrances' ('because' – offer this along with 'bee-cay-use', and the child won't find it confusing. He can remember either one or both, to make assurance double sure.) 'Never eat cheese, eat salmon sandwiches and remain young' for 'necessary'. I struggle to think of mnemonics on the spur of the moment, and my students are much better at it. They have suggested, for instance, 'cheese is rotten; can't like everything' ('circle' – picture a round and mouldy cheese), 'can old ladies dance' ('cold'), 'never eat weeds' ('new'). You would think they wouldn't remember them; but they thought of them, they remember them. With a satisfied smirk at their inventiveness. "Yes Miss, you can let the others have my mnemonic, of course you can."

Try to steer a child away from over enthusiasm in this direction, though.

Tell him to go for re-pronunciation if possible, and to keep that as close to the original as he can: simplest is best. Then he can save his mnemonic cannon for the real monsters.

What is the basic theme of the spelling campaign you and your child have undertaken together? It's this: you are changing the way he looks at print. Correct spelling has to begin with a close scrutiny of the words he sees: the re-routing has to start from A, not from B or C (see diagram on page 31). He must learn to examine words so as to decide, first of all, whether they *are* regular; and if not which are the sneaky bits, and what he is going to do about them.

This is the point of the *Alpha to Omega* programme, and why the authors think it is an approach to reading as well as spelling. They know that accurate spelling has to be rooted in the ability to read aloud accurately, and they also know that for many children, accurate reading aloud has to be rooted in phonics. The mistake they have made is to assume that reading aloud is the same as real reading. In fact 'phonic translation' has nothing whatever to do with real reading. A child may translate 'pond' into sounds, so as to discover the meaning; but then he has to go on and teach himself to 'really read' the word. He has to invest the pattern of shapes with the same meaning already inherent in the equivalent pattern of sounds: he has to see it as a transparent whole, and perceive the meaning through it. Noticing the sound for each letter is a hindrance at this point, not a help. The letters have to undergo a sea change, and become something entirely other. They have to flow together, a window onto pond-ness.

Children, of course, can manage this amazing feat easily, hardly aware of what they're doing. But, when they need to learn to spell the word, then they have to shift their focus back again. Once again they must look *at* the letters rather than through them, separating them, matching each one with a heard sound – with an uttered sound – with a felt movement of the pencil over a piece of paper. They need to practise 'phonic reading', not in order to understand the words, but so as to translate them, for whatever end they choose.

Once we make this clear distinction in our own minds, between 'real reading', and 'saying written words aloud', we can see that all children need to be able to operate both processes. Dyslexics particularly must learn to focus on the letters while they read, and the *Alpha to Omega* programme ensures that they do exactly that. But of the power and the glory of the world of real books, *Alpha to Omega* has nothing to say; a child who is given a diet of nothing else is poor indeed. Not to worry. He is learning to read in a different time and space altogether, bewitched by the authors of Liz Waterland's 'organic' books.

The weapons fall from our grasp, and we stare at each other across the trenches, wondering why we ever made such a fuss in the first place. Of course children need to do both, and of course our job is to work out the most effective ways of helping them. The only sensible action is to shake hands rather sheepishly, and get on with it.

A careful examination of written words, then, is important. When it is established, you can help your child to explore the insides of language even further, showing him how the building blocks of meaning come together in fresh and startling ways. We're not stupid, after all, and we're not particularly energetic either. As a new concept emerges, we don't bestir ourselves to create whole new words. We cut bits out of the ones we have inherited, and stitch them into new patterns. The Greeks decided to use 'phone' meaning 'sound', and 'tele' for 'a long distance'. Helping ourselves to both bits, we create the word 'telephone' for a marvel of modern technology. And 'television', 'telescope', 'microscope' . . . the list is endless.

We can attach a meaning block to the beginning of a word, when it becomes a pre-fix (fixed before); or tack it on to the other end – a suffix. The more you pay attention to prefixes and suffixes, the more interesting they become, so use the words 'prefix' and 'suffix' as handles for your child to think about them, and help him to notice them. Here is a list to get you started:

tele	=	from afar (telephone, telegraph, television, telescope)
phone	=	sound (telephone, linguaphone, phonic)
graph	=	visual shape, e.g. letters or pictures (graph, telegraph, graphics)
scope	=	view or observe (telescope, microscope)
un	=	not (undo)
re	=	again (redo)
ing	=	when you do something (standing)

ly	=	how you do something (cleverly)
er	=	more/one who (redder, banker)
est	=	the most (largest, best)
en	=	to make (lengthen, fasten, strengthen)
mis	=	wrong (misspell = to spell wrongly; misplace = to place wrongly: only one 's' because 'place' begins with 'p', not 's')

See the book *Lingo,* by Adrian Spooner (Bristol Classical Press) for lots of good ideas in this direction.

Now you can strengthen the repronunciation of many irregular words by pointing out the meanings of the different bits. The 'ed' suffix, for instance, hardly sounding in 'jumped', 'pushed', 'frightened', tells you nevertheless that something happened in the past. Last week, last month, or last year – but it isn't happening now. Saying 'jump-ĕd', 'push-ĕd' and 'frighten-ĕd' not only reminds you to include the silent 'e', but also links the meanings of these words with others where the 'e' is sounded: 'tasted', 'plaited', 'started'. You can use grammatical terms here, quite naturally – all doing or happening words are verbs, so 'ed' is a suffix attached to a verb.

Feeling your way around inside words, like this, is a fascinating undertaking. Words are powerful creatures. Over many years, human beings have laden them with the finest treasures of their minds, and children who take possession of them are taking possession of the world. One of my students, with severe spelling problems, and a real pain in mainstream lessons as a result, had a mum who never gave up. Between us, we seduced him into reading, and then re-routed his spelling. One morning it was Paul who was jumping up and down outside my car with news that wouldn't wait. "Miss, miss, *miss!*" The words came tumbling out. "You know that spelling test, that I got 29 on, I did it again with my mum last night and I got 57! 57!" "Paul, that's fantastic, that's brilliant, gosh, I'm so pleased." Whenever I saw him, for days afterwards, he nudged me and gloated, "Fifty seven!" and when the local bookshop put on a display in the school, the first book Paul reserved for himself was a dictionary. He had discovered that words didn't just belong to other people, they belonged to him too, every single one.

So help your child to fall in love with the magic and mystery of words.

It's an affair that will last a lifetime, and one he will never regret.

It will also provide clear, easy access to most of the school curriculum. Here I can't resist reporting on a rather neat little experiment I carried out recently.

Part of my brief, as a 'Special Education' teacher, is to support my strugglers in some of their mainstream lessons, so from time to time I stray into the Science block. My task was virtually impossible, though, when my strugglers were scattered among the groups, and at the end of one school year, I suggested that in September they should all be assigned to the same group. This idea was greeted with dismay, as a retrograde step. "We'll just be creating a sink group, Felicity, it will be impossible to teach, your lot will hold the others back." "No they won't, I promise, don't worry about them, don't make any concessions in terms of content, teach to the others, I'll worry about my ones." The Science team have learned by now that once I get hold of a scheme, I don't abandon it lightly, so they gave in with varying degrees of grace.

Come September, my eight second year strugglers formed nearly half of a small group of eighteen. (Their year was the first to show the effect of falling rolls.) The group were tackling electricity, with me beside them, trying to keep up, and wondering why science was never like this when I was at school. The lessons were brilliantly conducted, including a nice balance of discussion, explanation and practical work. Even I could understand most of what went on.

After about ten weeks, we were warned that there would be a test the following week, so I wheedled five minutes out of the teacher, and spread nine different terms across the blackboard. Circuit, series, parallel, conductor, insulator, resistor, variable resistor, diode, ammeter. "There you are," I said to the class, "nine words – and they cover all the science you've been doing for the last ten weeks. Copy them down, go over them really thoroughly before the test, and you're certain to pass at the very least."

Naturally I didn't leave it there as far as my strugglers were concerned. I had the eight in small extraction groups over the next few days, and we turned that list of words inside out. I wrote the words in each child's vocabulary book, and went over them one by one.

"Meanings first – what's a circuit? You must be precise, not vague – didn't we use the word 'path' in the lesson? Right, it's a path that electricity travels around. I'll write the word 'path' in small letters in your notebook, to remind you. Now – what's a 'series circuit' – how many paths for the electricity? Only one, good – let's write 'how many paths?' beside the word 'series', to remind ourselves, and then I'll add a 1. And I'll draw a tiny diagram, as well. What happens if you break the circuit? – yes, all the lights go out, like Christmas tree lights, because the electricity can't get through. So what about a 'parallel circuit'? – we'll ask the same question, what's the answer? Two or more paths, well done. Turn off one light, and the rest do what? Stay on, of course.

"The next five terms all name things that do something to electricity, so we'll bracket them together. What does a conductor do?" I had covered that lesson for Colin-the-Science during his absence, and took care to put the emphasis on the relevant words. The memory needed only a bit of stirring. "It leads something, Miss – oh yes, it lets the electricity through." "Well done – how about an insulator, then?" "It's the opposite, Miss, it stops it." "That's right, do you remember what the 'insula' bit means? And the 'tor' bit?" "Yes, 'tor' means something that does . . ." but they drew a blank on 'insula'. I hadn't realized the connection before I looked up the word, but of course an 'insulator' is a material that can be wrapped around another substance to turn it into an island! "Let's write 'island' in tiny letters over this 'insula' bit, to remind you." "Yes I remember now, Miss, like Britain – the invaders can't get at us." "Right, because the sea's an insulator. How about a 'resistor' – do you remember when I pretended to drag Katrina out of the classroom, and she resisted, she tried to stop me? So a resistor *tries* to stop the electricity, but it doesn't quite succeed. Here's the symbol for 'resistor', look. And a variable resistor?" "It tries harder sometimes, Miss, but sometimes it stops just a bit, when you turn the knob – and you put a line across the symbol to show the knob." "We're doing amazingly well here – what about 'diode'? Let's look up the prefix 'di' in the dictionary, it means 'two', look, how is that part of 'di-ode'?" Pause for thought, then: "We put it two ways, Miss, one way it stopped it, and the other way it didn't."

"You're going to do brilliantly on this test, you know, only one word left, 'ammeter'. What does the 'meter' bit mean?" "It measures – it measures amps, that's the 'am' at the front." "And what are amps – oh yes, they're the amount of current, aren't they?

"We're running out of time, but we'll just whizz through the list again, and I'll suggest some memory boosters. When you go over the words at home you can decide whether to use the same ones, or think of new ones. 'Circuit' – how about 'ker-koo-it' – will you remember the 'i' at the beginning, that's a bit sneaky, go over that . . . Now, Wednesday night, just half an hour, practise writing the words as well, I want them coming out of your *ears* on Thursday."

The test was a good one, quite searching, not just a matter of recall. Colin read it through quickly to the whole group, and anyone was allowed to flap a hand and ask me to re-read a difficult part, in whispers. Both strugglers and 'non' strugglers availed themselves of this, but only to a limited extent. For the most part, the group worked confidently, on their own. When they'd finished, they all swapped papers, Colin went over the answers, and they marked each other's work.

Finally the marks were recorded. I listened with a gathering grin. One of the group was absent, leaving nine 'more able' students, and my eight. There were one or two fairly low marks, but not from my strugglers. Four of the 'more able' students scored below 50% (49%, 47%, 45% and 34%). All my lot reported half marks at least, and several were considerably higher. The average percentage for the 'more able' students was 53%, but for my strugglers 65%. The three top marks in the whole group were recorded by three of mine, 85%, 75% and 71% respectively.

At the end of the lesson, I couldn't resist a quick aside. "Who's holding who back, Colin?" I asked sweetly. He was unrepentant. "Very interesting to see how that test identified the bright ones," he remarked, hoping I would rise to the bait. I decided to be magnanimous in victory, and humour him. "Hasn't it dawned on you yet, Colin? They're *all* bright. It's just that with some of them, we haven't yet succeeded in cleaning down to the shine." "Oh well," he responded smiling. "I suppose you want them *all* to have vocabulary books now? And for us to pick out a couple of key words each lesson? Yes, I thought you would. Okay – why not?"

The power of words – to unlock whole trains of thought, whole areas of experience. But you have to get inside them first.

You need only a small notebook, for recording your 'sneak' collection. Now my strugglers take the notebook to all their lessons, and write down the important and useful words, maybe one or two, from a session. (The words

51

are listed in chronological order, not divided up alphabetically, or by subject, although the subject is noted beside each group of words.) "Every night," I say, "use your new words to help you tell your mums and dads about what went on in your lessons. Then go through the whole collection, first for meanings, then for the memory boosters. Spend a couple of minutes, no more. That'll keep all the spellings – *and* all the ideas – at the front of your heads. After a bit, when you really know a page, you can drop that one and concentrate on the more recent ones. When you come to study for a test, go over the words for that subject, alongside your exercise book. It's a beautifully simply way of organizing yourself."

It is, and it works.

VII

Some 'help' sheets for parents and peer tutors

First, a general 'Spelling Instruction Sheet' for parents:

THE APPRENTICESHIP APPROACH

A Spelling Instruction Sheet

1. Show your child how to tally written words with sounds, by demonstrating the procedure when you're reading with him. (See Book Two)
2. One day, choose a shortish, interesting, regular word; and when he has tallied it, ask him to tally it again, from memory. So, for 'frog', he will say 'fŭ, frŭ, frŏ, frog', without looking. (Any time he gets in a muddle, just repeat the sounds correctly for him, until he gets them right. You're not testing him, you're showing him.)
3. Ask him to tally the word again, silently, and to spell the word out loud, thinking of the matching sound each time. So when he thinks 'fu', he says 'f'; he thinks 'fru' and adds the 'r'; 'fro' and says 'o'; 'frog' and says 'g'. (This procedure, once mastered, will go a long way towards anchoring the spellings of many words, in the proper order, in his mind. Keep on practising it with him, tackling different regular words, until it comes easily. Praise him, and remind him of his growing ability, all the time.)
4. Encourage him to use words he has already tallied, and spelled orally, in his writing. Now he should tally the word to himself while he writes. Start 'talking' him through' the spellings of regular words if he asks for help when he's writing.
5. Begin to choose 'irregular' words from the reading you do together, for

53

his oral spelling sessions. Tackle just one word a day, to begin with. Tally it first, and then decide on a memory booster, or mnemonic, which will help to anchor the spelling. Record the words in a spelling notebook, for easy reference.

It's better to do this by the date, rather than alphabetically, then you can see how much ground you have covered in a given period, and easily review the memory boosters learned so far. I usually group the words in twos – much less daunting than a page long list. Some words need to be grouped in larger clumps, though; notice the handy way of remembering 'hear' and 'heard', and distinguishing these from the 'here, there and everywhere' words:

Date	Word	Memory Booster
7.5.87	suddenly	sud - den - ly
	snake	snak - e
		(magic 'e' word)
9.5.87	ear	
	hear	what you do with your ear
	heard	h - ear - d
		(what you did with your ear)
	here	here (in this place)
	there	t - here (in that place)
	where	w - here (in what place)
	their	belonging to them
16.5.87	light	l - indians get hot - t
	information	in - for - ma - ti - on
21.5.87	which	w - hich
	cheap	che - ap
13.6.87	trotting	trot - ting
		(double 'defence' rule)
24.6.87	fright	fr - indians get hot - t
	frighten	fright - en (to make afraid)
	frightened	fright - en - ed (happened in the past)

54

The basic theme of my work is that becoming literate is simply a matter of forming the relevant associations. A child needs to form an infinite number of associations between patterns of shapes and meanings. He also needs to associate patterns of shapes with other kinds of patterns: heard sounds, vocal sensations, handwriting movements.

And that's it. It boils down to nothing more than practice. A child doesn't have to 'reinvent' the English written system, which is the task often thrust upon him in the past. He just has to have the abundant experience of using it. There is no question that he has the mental capacity to form all these associations, because exactly the same kinds of associations are involved in learning to hear and to speak.

Our job, as mediators of literacy, is to work out how to provide the essential practice, and we need to tackle this in two main ways. The first is to appreciate the organic nature of written language, and how the different literacy processes grow and unfold out of each other. Seeing the meanings in written words comes first, then seeing the matching sounds, with ever increasing precision; and this in turn leads on to the ability to reproduce written words yourself. Much of our literacy teaching has gone awry in the past, not because we were teaching the wrong things, but just that we were introducing them in the wrong order. We were expecting children to become accomplished cyclists before they had even realized that the wheels went round, or that whizzing along on a bicycle was a fun thing to do!

Our second task is a practical one. The very best way of providing the necessary experience is by means of one-to-one help; which is why parents are ideal literacy teachers, and this series is written primarily for them. Maybe one day we will reach the point where all children become literate at home in their first five years of life, quite naturally and 'unconsciously'. Then when they get to school their teachers can have a whale of a time leading them on a myriad journeys of exploration, using either form of language to enrich and illuminate their passage.

Ah well. In the meantime we have to rack our brains, figuring out how to arrange one-to-one help for children who haven't got there yet, in the seemingly impossible context of a school organization!

This is how my own role, at Dartmouth Community College, has developed. Thanks to a hugely supportive deputy head, and a very positive English department, I have now reached the point where I work almost entirely alongside the timetable, extracting some children from some English lessons, for extra input, and supporting them in other curriculum areas. This has extended to a perception that I am responsible for the literacy 'infrastructure' throughout the school, trying to make good areas of weakness wherever they occur. All the time I am discovering 'how to do it' on a one-to-one basis. Then I pass my findings on to parents; and hammer out, with the English team, ways of incorporating the ideas in mainstream lessons. The continual feedback from parents, teachers and children is invaluable. Children especially never flannel you. If a particular technique demolishes the barriers for them they will jump up and down for joy. But equally they will be the first to let you know when they are less than enthusiastic about a programme. "Do I really have to do all this stuff Miss? It's dead boring!" (Back to the drawing board and the search for another channel to success.)

It's quite easy to crack the reading, even at secondary level. You just lay your hands on as many delicious books as you can, by fair means or foul, and rope in all available parents, relatives, volunteers, technology and other children to provide the reading input. Piece of cake.

The writing and spelling are more difficult, and I made several false starts in this area. I knew roughly what I wanted to do, but to begin with I got the order wrong, and then for quite a while couldn't see how to delegate to other tutors.

The order fooled me because, like many people, I assumed that to solve the spelling problem, you had to begin by showing kids ways of dealing with 'irregular' words, with the sneaks. These were the real bugbears, and I was mightily pleased with myself as my system of memory boosters emerged. 'Re-pronounce' the sneaks, in one way or another, and you had the thing licked.

I didn't. As always, it was my work with Edward that made me think again. I spent ages showing Edward how to use memory boosters, and only gradually realized that *none of it was registering*. After months of effort, his spelling was just as abysmal as it had always been. What was going wrong?

It dawned on me that I had to start off showing Edward how to spell *regular* words. Of course he couldn't tackle the sneaks straightaway, as most of my other students could. I was much too far ahead of where he was.

Because he didn't read aloud, he had no idea how to match regular words with sounds, and so use the procedure as a way of bypassing the visualizing blockage.

At this point, my rediscovery of *Alpha to Omega* was an eye opener, not just because it showed me the way ahead for Edward. I realized as I examined it that many of my other students were a bit vague about how to spell regular words. They had annexed some of the territory for themselves, which was why I hadn't been fully aware of their struggles. But their command was still patchy. I could see now that most poor spellers would benefit from the strong framework in spelling regular words provided by this useful little book. So my next job was to work out how to enable students in mainstream English lessons to use it to plug the gaps.

To begin with, I got carried away by enthusiasm. Some of the relevant practice involved in literacy is practice in writing accurately: writing in sentences, using punctuation appropriately, spelling correctly. If children have reached secondary level without sufficient experience of accurate writing, it is quite difficult to ensure that they get it. *Alpha to Omega* seemed to offer a solution to this problem as well. Many exercises consist of 'Sentences for dictation'. How about arranging for the poor spellers to dictate these sentences to themselves, tallying the words, thinking about the punctuation and what it meant, writing neatly, and then proofreading and correcting what they had written? They could work at their own pace and so would be free to concentrate on neatness and accuracy rather than quantity. Gradually these habits of accuracy would take root and spread across to their creative and independent work.

Well, that was the theory, and for some children it worked. But even though the instructions were to decide for themselves how much of each exercise to do, many poor spellers in mainstream classes became very bogged down in the apparently endless acres of sentences. They couldn't see where it was all leading, and rebelled.

There is never any sense in making children do something they really don't want to. I tried to keep on explaining the point of the thing. "I know it sounds daft, but it's *supposed* to be boring. I don't for one minute mean I want to give you boring things to do for the good of your soul! When you're reading books, and writing poems and stories, I want you to be passionately interested in what you're doing. But if you got all involved in what these sentences are *about*, you would be too busy thinking about the meanings to concentrate on the writing and spelling. The exercises aren't interesting, but if you keep on with them you will find that they're satisfying." Again, this worked with some children, but others refused to be bamboozled, and abandoned the programme.

Meanwhile, I was becoming quite overwhelmed, trying to provide all necessary input for my severe strugglers. I wanted to carry on tasting books with them, to get them hooked on new authors, keep tabs on their *Alpha to Omega* work, help them with memory boosters for their mainstream vocabularies – there just weren't enough hours in the day. If only I could clone myself in several directions at once I might have a chance. Some hope.

It was about this time that I went to a day's course on peer tutoring at Exeter University, conducted by Keith Topping, an educational psychologist who is based at Kirklees Metropolitan Council, Huddersfield, West Yorkshire. He has carried out a great deal of research into helping children help each other, in virtually all areas of the curriculum, and has found, unsurprisingly, that peer tutoring is highly effective, not least for the tutors themselves. (Learn something well enough to teach it, and you are several stages further on than just being generally aware of a smattering of information drifting across your head.)

I was already familiar with his work on paired reading – I've explained both my reservations and support for this in Book One. I knew that children sharing books with children were an excellent reinforcement for parents and other adults sharing books with children. I had assumed, though, that monitoring my individuals' *Alpha to Omega* work, and explaining about memory boosters, was something only I could do.

Keith Topping, it emerged, had other ideas. One of his talks was about 'cued spelling'. All my ears pricked when I realized cued spelling was exactly my own 'memory booster' approach, but with a different terminology. And masses of children were teaching cued spelling to masses of children with no trouble at all. We saw videos to prove it. Of course children could teach it to each other. Who better?

I liked his terminology very much. Whereas I had talked about 'splitting-a-word-into-bits', Keith Topping said, "Chunk it." Chunk it. Lovely, Because 'chunk' is both noun and verb, you can not only explain the action, you can also refer to particular 'chunks'. Why hadn't I thought of that?

And, instead of 'memory boosters' or 'mnemonics' – simply 'cues'. You show a child how to decide on cues for a word, and this can be either re-pronunciation, or a mnemonic, or a mixture of the two. Again, the term 'cues' enables you to be much more helpful in your instructions to a child. A 'memory booster' covers a whole word, whereas a 'cue' can home in on just one 'chunk'.

I adopted Keith Topping's terminology on the spot.

More solutions appeared. An important part of the cued spelling programme was writing the words. So if I introduced cued spelling at Dartmouth, via peer tutors, then maybe I could cut down on the writing involved in the *Alpha to Omega* programme. If that became largely oral, with the emphasis on practice in reading aloud, I could whizz my strugglers through it more quickly, maintaining their involvement and momentum by giving them rapid success in the three tests (one at the end of each stage). They would still have a fair amount of writing practice overall, but would cover much more territory at a bound, so they wouldn't get bogged down. *And I could use peer tutors to teach that as well!*

I flew home and spent the weekend rethinking. These redrafted 'help' sheets are what emerged. We are using them both in mainstream lessons, for anyone who needs them, and with small extraction groups: initial results have been very encouraging.

Since the heart of peer tutoring is the same one-to-one approach that is central to the apprenticeship philosophy, it doesn't matter if the 'tutor' is a parent, or another child. But the first sheet is specifically for parents who are helping their child to use the *Alpha to Omega* spelling programme, for the first time.

When in doubt about which stage is right for your child, give him one of the three tests provided in the book, and refer to the mark scheme at the bottom. If you start a child on Stage II, review some of the key ideas from Stage I, first. I talk about 'vowel sandwiches' quite a bit, which seems to tickle a child's fancy – these are the three letter words with a consonant at either end, and the short vowel sound in the middle. Then you can add further bits of bread to both sides, building from 'ram' to 'cram' to 'cramp', for instance. Finally, a magic 'e' tacked on to a vowel sandwich makes the vowel sound long. Then just about covers Stage I!

For the cued spelling, I suggest you tackle six words, chosen by your child, each week, and aim at three short sessions per week. Session 1: first three words. Session 2: second three words. Session 3: review words for week.

If you want to find out more about peer tutoring, *The Peer Tutoring Handbook*, by Keith Topping, is published by Croom Helm. An abundant supply of materials, including, for instance, an excellent video showing children tutoring each other in cued spelling, and a cued spelling diary for monitoring progress, is available from: The Paired Learning Project, Oastler Centre, 103 New Street, Huddersfield HD1 2UA, West Yorkshire.

THE APPRENTICESHIP APPROACH

SPELLING PROGRAMME – ALPHA TO OMEGA

1. Work through the Stage in order, but skip if you feel this is sensible.
2. For a long exercise (more than ten sentences) do two sentences
   less than ten sentences – do one sentence.
3. Work in pencil (lead HB). Keep a plastic rubber handy (doesn't smudge). Use joined writing. (This helps the fingers to remember the spellings.)
4. Use a step by step approach, but leave out steps as your child gains confidence.

DO NOT RUSH

QUALITY NOT SPEED

EVERY SENTENCE MUST BE PERFECT

FOLLOW THESE STEPS:

a) Help your child to read any lists of words. Tally if necessary. Make it fun, and offer plenty of encouragement.
b) Go on to the exercise. Help your child to read all the sentences aloud. He reads each sentence for meaning, silently, first. Then he goes back to the beginning and reads it aloud. Help him whenever he gets stuck.
c) Dictate the sentence(s) word by word. Say the first word. Your child spells it orally. *You* write it down, in joined writing, commenting on the height and length of the letters, the joins and connectors.
   Your child writes the word out of his head. Remind him to hold the spoken word in his mind, and match the letters against it. Rub out any mistakes, until the word is perfect.
   Remind about punctuation.
   When the sentence is complete, your child reads his sentence aloud.

d) When starting a session, ask your child to read aloud some or all of the sentences he has written so far.

e) After a while, your child can work on his own for part of the time. He copies first word by word, then two or three words at a time, then a whole sentence at a time. He must proofread every sentence (aloud if necessary) to make sure it is correct.

Then we're cracking it!

SPELLING PROGRAMME CHECK LIST

ALPHA TO OMEGA – STAGE I

Topic	Page	
Short vowel sounds	18	☐
Vowel sandwiches	19-23	☐
Consonant blends	24-28	☐
'N' before . . .	30-32	☐
Word sums	32-33	☐
'Ng', 'ngk'	34-36	☐
Verb endings	37	☐
'Ar' + word sums	37-40	☐
'Or' and 'er' + word sums	42-45	☐
The 'w' and 'qu' rules	46-50	☐
Short forms etc.	52-54	☐
'Al' saying 'aw'	54-56	☐
'Ff' words	61-62	☐
'Ck' words	63-66	☐
Vowel – consonant – e		
a – e	69-71	☐
i – e	73-74	☐
o – e	74-76	☐
u – e	76-77	☐
More lazy 'e' words	78	☐
The 'v' rule	80-81	☐
'Tch'	96-97	☐
Stage I Spelling Test	99 (See me)	☐

SPELLER

1. Read all lists of words *aloud* (to yourself).
2. Learn lists of odd words. (Decide on cues.)
3. Sentences for dictation –   Read *all* sentences aloud (to yourself).

   More than 10 sentences – copy out 2 sentences. (Copy word by word. Use LOOK, SAY, COVER, WRITE, CHECK.)

   Less than 10 sentences – copy out 1 sentence.
4. Ask helper to assess your work.

HELPER

1. Speller reads list of words to you.
2. Choose 3 words from list – Speller tallies word on page.
   Speller tallies word from memory.
   Speller spells word aloud.
3. Speller reads *half* the sentences in each exercise. (You choose the sentences.)
4. Mark speller's sentences.
5. Check his corrections.
6. If you are satisfied, put 'S' and your initials on speller's checklist.
7. If you are not satisfied, speller reviews section, you reassess.

NAME _____

SPELLING PROGRAMME CHECK LIST

ALPHA TO OMEGA – STAGE II

<u>Topic</u>   <u>Page</u>

Long 'ā' sound   100-104   ☐
Long 'ō' sound   104-106   ☐
Long 'ū' sound   106-110   ☐
Long 'ī' sound   111-113   ☐
Long 'ē' sound   113-118   ☐
'Ea' saying 'ā'   118-120   ☐
Letter writing – informal letter   120 (See me)   ☐
                    formal letter   120 (See me)   ☐
'Ea' saying 'ĕ'   121-122   ☐
'Oi' and 'oy' ('Come here' sound)   122-124   ☐
'Ouch' sound   124-127   ☐
'Aw' sound   128-130   ☐
'Ir' and 'ur'   131-132   ☐
'Ear' saying 'er'   132-134   ☐
Punctuation passages   138 (See me)   ☐
Magic rules* – find the matching rule in Spelling Programme
                (139-147) and learn the examples. (See me).   ☐
Learn Rules V, VI, VII   147-152   ☐
Plurals   152-156   ☐
Stage II Spelling Test   157 (See me)   ☐

* *These are the six magic rules given in Book Two, Section IX.*

65

SPELLER

1. Learn the different ways of spelling the sound.
2. Read the lists of words aloud (to yourself). Notice sneaks, decide on cues, and learn them.
3. Learn lists of odd words. (Decide on cues.)
4. Sentences for dictation – More than 10 sentences – copy out 2 sentences. (Copy word by word. Use LOOK, SAY, COVER WRITE CHECK.)

   Less than 10 sentences – copy out 1 sentence.
5. Ask helper to mark your work.
6. Correct your work. Ask helper to check.
7. Ask helper to test you.

HELPER

When speller has finished a section:
1. Mark speller's sentences.
2. Check his corrections.
3. Test him orally on:
   i) different ways of spelling the sound
   ii) lists of words (choose some examples from each list)
   iii) lists of odd words
4. If you are satisfied, put 'S' and your initials on speller's checklist.
5. If you are not satisfied, speller reviews section, you retest.

SPELLING PROGRAMME

ALPHA TO OMEGA – STAGE III

1. Read through Spelling Test on p. 216.
2. Skim through Stage III. Decide which sections you want to learn (as for Stage II).
3. Make your own checklist. List sections (and pages).
    E.g. 'Ph' saying 'f', p. 187.
    Advanced prefixes and suffixes, p. 211.
    Latin and Greek prefixes and suffixes, pp. 212-213.
4. Show me list.
5. Learn the chosen sections. Use some of the words in written sentences.
5. Learn Stage III Spelling Test, using cued spelling.
6. Take Stage III Spelling Test, p. 216. Aim at 100% correct!
7. Apply to the university of your choice.

HELPER

When speller has finished a section:
1. Speller reads lists of words to you.
2. Choose 5 words from list. Speller tallies word on page.

    Speller thinks of cues if necessary.

    Speller either – tallies word from memory

    or – says cues.

    Speller spells word aloud.
3. If you are satisfied, put 'S' and your initials on speller's checklist.
4. If you are not satisfied, speller reviews section, you reassess.

ALPHA TO OMEGA SPELLING PROGRAMME

A Marking Guide - Helpers

1. Use a different coloured pen.
2. Refer to the original sentence.
3. Underline any errors in your partner's work. (Do *not* write in the correction.) Put a small cross in the margin for each error. Look out for errors in punctuation and handwriting, as well as spelling.
4. When speller has corrected all errors, score out the crosses, and put a tick to the left of the crosses.
5. If some errors have not been corrected, speller must correct them before you give him a tick!
6. All errors must be corrected before you are 'satisfied'.

A Correcting Guide – Spellers

1. Notice all underlinings.
2. Read all marked words aloud (to yourself). This will help you to see the errors.
3. Think about punctuation errors. Think about what punctuation signs mean. (Punctuation signs are signals to help you read aloud sensibly. E.g. A full stop tells you to pause at the end of a complete idea. A comma signals a shorter pause, but the meaning keeps on going. A question mark tells your voice to go up. And so on.)
4. Refer to the original.
5. Rub out errors and write in corrections, in pencil.
6. Check your corrections against the original.

CUED SPELLING

10 STEPS

1. SPELLER CHOOSES WORD (from his vocabulary notebook).

2. SPELLER CHECKS CORRECT SPELLING.
   HELPER CHECKS CORRECT SPELLING.

3. HELPER AND SPELLER BOTH READ THE WORD ALOUD.

4. SPELLER CHOOSES CUES.

5. HELPER AND SPELLER SAY CUES TOGETHER.

6. SPELLER SAYS CUES.
   HELPER WRITES WORD (in cursive handwriting).

7. HELPER SAYS CUES.
   SPELLER WRITES WORD (in cursive handwriting).

8. SPELLER SAYS CUES AND WRITES WORD AGAIN.

9. SPELLER WRITES WORD FAST.

10. SPELLER READS WORD.

4 RULES

1. Helper covers previous tries.
2. Speller checks his own try.
3. Helper does not tell speller he is wrong, or correct spelling.
   He says (e.g.) "I'm not sure about that – I suggest you look at that again."
4. Helper praises.

2 REVIEWS

1. *Speed Review*
   Speller writes all words for day FAST, and checks. For any wrong words, the 10 steps are repeated.

2. *Master Review*

Speller writes all words for week FAST, and checks. He decides what to do about wrong words – e.g. carry them forward to the following week.

Suggested cues

1. 'Chunk' the word into bits, and repronounce each bit so as to turn it into a regular word.

E.g.   Wed-nes-day

                      dee-ki-si-on (decision)

Think of a mnemonic for all or part of a word.

E.g.   Big elephants can't always use small entrances (because).

Cats always use great heavy toilets (caught).

Little apes sit and gobble nuts energetically (lasagne).

People need electric umbrellas – monia (pneumonia).

Queens undress everywhere so they're in our news (question).

Big elephants aren't ugly – tiful (beautiful).

Some people eat crabs in a lavatory (special).

Cannibals always use little drums – ron (cauldron).

Ghosts hate oranges, sausages, tea (ghost).

Giant rabbits are pretty hopeless skippers (graphs).

Never eat cheese, eat salmon sandwiches and remain young (necessary).

Old uncles get heavy/hypothermia (ough).

Old uncles like driving (ould).

All unicorns grow horns (augh).

Indians get hot (igh).

VIII

Typewriters and computers

One of the attractions of my Special Ed room is that it boasts three typewriters and two computers, all readily accessible to the children. No other room on the lower site has these advantages, so naturally children gravitate towards it. (I'm not stupid, I believe in carrots and rewards and shameless bribery. 'Special' education should be exactly that.) Nearly all children are keen on learning to type. They think they are mastering an impressive, grown up and marketable skill, which indeed they are. The main reason I want them to learn to touchtype, however, is that it helps them to spell. 'Spelling is learned in the fingertips', and a child who has learned the sequence his fingers must perform in order to type a word correctly, has yet another way of remembering its spelling.

A friend comes in voluntarily, three times a week, to help the students learn to type. She is herself a skilful typist and computer operator, and increasingly fascinated by the hidden talents my strugglers possess. Often, I will hear her remark, "Robert, you may not know how to spell this word, but your fingers do. See that finger going to the 'i', it knows what comes next." Robert looks at his fingers in amazement. How can they possibly know something that he does not? But they do.

This is why it is a good idea to learn to touchtype, on a manual typewriter, before becoming too familiar with a computer keyboard. It is easy to become proficient with a computer using random fingering – the important thing is what is happening on the screen, not what your fingers are doing. But try to learn to touchtype, once you are whizzing away on computers, and it is virtually impossible. (I know, I tried to teach fifth year Ashley to touchtype, feeling this would be a powerful weapon in his spelling armoury. But he was already such a grand master of the computer keyboard that he found the totally different technique, necessary to touchtype, very frustrating. After a few sessions we both abandoned the attempt, heaving sighs of relief.) If you are already an expert touchtypist, however, it is a straightforward matter to transfer these skills from typewriter to computer.

Type it[8] is a helpful teaching manual, designed specifically for children with spelling problems. (It incorporates a goodly amount of phonic drills, so furnishing a relatively agreeable way of practising these; and the student starts typing whole words, rather than strings of letters, almost immediately.) Many students have taught themselves to type, after an initial explanatory session with me, using this manual.

A nicer way of beginning, with a child not yet self motivated, is to choose a poem he has written, often one he has dictated to you. Write all the correct lettering on the child's fingers (the middle knuckle, so they can be easily seen), and sit beside him while he types out his composition. You dictate it back to him, telling him the spacing and punctuation, and any spellings he needs. (You are allowed to paint out mistakes with typewriter correcting fluid!) He can look at the keyboard all he wishes. Typing by touch alone will come later. But he still has the feeling of using the right fingers, and the experience of producing a perfect piece of work, his own ideas in his own language. When he has finished, he illustrates it, and his creation is pinned up on the wall all for everyone to see and admire. (Better to begin with a poem, rather than a story, because it's shorter. You want to give your child the feeling of success as quickly as possible.

You may see a snag at this point. You cannot type. (Many parents can type, though, and are unaware what a useful skill this is to pass on to their children.) Invest in a secondhand typewriter, and teach yourself. It doesn't take long, and your child will be delighted to feel that you are mastering a skill alongside him, just for his benefit; you may well reap some benefits yourself, of course.

Computers offer a different kind of experience, and different rewards. They can take the place of another adult in the classroom, providing one-to-one attention, or motivating a child with the strongest possible incentives to understand the written language appearing on the screen. Some discs encourage children to work together, helping one another to find their way through a maze of puzzles and problems. The immortal 'Granny's Garden' does all three, and is popular right up the age range.[9] (Even the cleaning lady got hooked one afternoon, when the students had gone, and abandoned her bucket and cloths to see if she could escape the witch's clutches *this* time!) Another useful disc, similarly addictive, is 'Thirteen Programmes', available from Dorset County Council, County Treasurer's Department, County Hall, Dorchester, Dorset DT1 1XJ. This gives much useful and delightful practice in disentangling left from right, or predicting what letters to choose for words and sentences, to save you from being devoured by the monster lurking hungrily in his den. My favourite is called 'Sound-snap', and involves moving a vowel muncher around the screen, eating the appropriate vowels when a picture of an apple, elephant, indian, octopus or umbrella is shown. Children with visualizing problems often have particular difficulty choosing the right vowels, because the matching sounds are fairly similar, and this programme helps to distinguish them.

Once a child has become familiar with computers, he can venture out into the territory of programming them himself, which is not that difficult, even for a mere adult like me. (I used to think it was quite beyond my scope, until I came across *The Usborne First Guide to the BBC Micro*,[10] a delightful cartoon style book written for primary school children. I sat down with it one day and produced coloured letters that danced across the screen, a dog wagging its tail, and a cacophony of sound effects ranging from a police siren to footsteps getting louder and louder. Very encouraging!) This sort of exploration is a great confidence booster for children, who begin to realize they are after all effective and in command.

Word processing is another area where computers are in the business of providing experience of success. A story or poem can be arranged and rearranged on the screen to the child's satisfaction, and then printed. He can design graphics to go with it. Discs enabling work to be shown in large clear letters on the screen are available; concept keyboards allow children to compose directly, without having to worry about spelling.

Persistently and powerfully, computers can help even a struggler to feel he is someone who can, rather than someone who can't.

Footnotes

8. By Joan Duffy, published by Better Books.

9. Available from: 4mation Educational Resources, Linden Lea, Rock Park, Barnstaple, Devon EX32 9AQ.

10. Usborne Publishing.

IX

The bright side of the spelling problem

Now I take a Lower School Assembly every year, aimed at the incoming first years. The second years have heard it all before, but this enables them to look knowing and superior when I launch into my spiel. The first years are unsuspecting.

"Why do you suppose," I ask them, "that you have two eyes? Why shouldn't one be enough? Try covering up one eye, and see if it makes a difference." Obediently, they do so, and then remove their hands, so that what they see takes on depth and solidity once more. "Did you notice," I say, "that everything looked rather flat and uninteresting when you were looking with only one eye? It was difficult to judge distance, wasn't it. But when you were using both eyes, things stood out again. That's the reason we have two eyes, so we can see 'in the round'.

"All of us can see objects 'in the round' when we're looking at them with two eyes, but of course when we visualize, inside our heads, everything looks flat, as if we were seeing it with just one mental eye. We don't need to visualize in three dimensions, the way we do when we're seeing real things.

"Hang on though, it would be quite useful. If you could also visualize in three dimensions, you might have all sorts of abilities most people don't possess. Think of modelling, or sculpture. Have you noticed that when you move round a piece of sculpture, it looks entirely different each time you stop? It would be handy to visualize like that, wouldn't it? Or architecture – if you could see in your mind's eye just how the different blocks of space went together, you would probably be ace at designing buildings. Or drawing, especially drawing in perspective – technical drawing – or designing computer programme – or playing chess, when it's an advantage to be able to visualize the relationships between the pieces, several moves further on. Or fiddling around with electronic gadgets – or playing tennis –

or whatever.

"Well, you may be interested to know that there are special people who can do exactly that. They *can* visualize 'in the round', and they're often very talented in one or more of the ways I've just mentioned. The most brilliant human being who ever lived, Albert Einstein, could see things in his mind in this way; and so could Winston Churchill, who was one of the greatest leaders our country has had. What's more, it's likely there are some of these special people in the room right now.

"Before you start getting excited, wondering if you are one of these talented individuals, I have to tell you that there is a snag. There always is, isn't there. Nothing can be had for nothing. The snag is that this ability to visualize in three dimensions *also happens with written words*. And that is a real pest. You could be looking at a word, inside your head – and the end of the word curls back on itself and turns up in the middle, back to front! Or the beginning could do the same thing. Or bits of it could roll over, and appear upside down.

"Think about the difficulties this can cause. You're likely to have real problems with reading, because it's an uphill struggle to recognize words. The word in your head doesn't match the word on the page at all. So if you're asked to read aloud, in class, you go all hot and embarrassed and wish you could just disappear. Spelling is even worse. You may be able to see a word, inside your head, in any number of different ways; and you have no idea which is the right one. If you ask the teacher for a spelling, you know your mates are going to look at you scornfully, and probably poke fun at you. "Don't you even know how to spell *that*? My sister can spell that, and she's only six!"

"Try to imagine, for a moment or two, what it must feel like to be someone with this different way of visualizing. You *know* you're just as good as anybody else really, you know you've got all this talent and potential, but every time you have to read and write, other people are going to think you're stupid. It's not surprising, is it, that some children just explode with frustration, and throw tables and chairs around if they think they are being made fun of.

"You may be surprised to hear that it's quite possible to learn to read and write very well indeed, even if written words are being complete and utter pests, but it takes time. Anyway, that's my job – I'm the Special Education teacher, and if you're 'special', in this way, I shall try to borrow you from some of your lessons, and give you as much help as I can with reading and writing. I'm in the room at the end, with the typewriters and computers, and we usually manage to have a lot of fun during our sessions.

"Suppose you don't need to work with me – why am I telling you all this? What can you do? I'm talking to you now because I badly need your help. If one of your classmates gets stuck when he's reading out loud, don't make fun of him or imply tht he's stupid. (He may well be much cleverer than you in many ways.) You could just supply the word that he needs, if that seems like a good idea. Or, if he asks for a spelling, tell him without any fuss. Remember that Einstein and Churchill couldn't spell for toffee! If he's away for a lesson, because he's working with me, tell him what he's missed when he gets back, the way you would if he'd missed an episode of *East Enders.* Notice the things he does well, and try to remark on them sometimes, so that he feels appreciated.

"And later on, when he's left school and perhaps become a brilliant artist, or sculptor, or scientist, or computer programmer, or chess player – you can say to yourself, 'I didn't make school miserable for him, I didn't get in his way, I helped.'"

Interesting things happen after these assemblies. Children flag me down in the corridor excitedly. "Miss – that's *just* how I see words. And I like drawing, and chess, and I can't spell. Can I come to your sessions? Can I learn to type?" "Oh, I wish everyone could learn to type. I tell you what, if I can't fit you in during lesson time, come along one lunch time and I'll start you off." They do, and they hang around when the bell rings, wishing they could stay. And my 'special' children, the ones who do stay, grow a few inches. 'Special' begins to mean exactly that. Or, one of my students tries to smuggle in a friend. "Miss, Jody's handwriting is rotten, can't he come with me?" Jody nods enthusiastically, eying the typewriters and computers with eager longing. "It's true Miss, I'm rubbish at handwriting, please can I come?" I have to chuckle, but it can't be done, not during lesson time, not just for handwriting. "But if you come back one evening, with Mum or Dad, the three of us could work together, if you want." Sometimes they do want, and they come. I tell the head of English, in passing, that I'm no longer trying to integrate Special Education into the mainstream. What I really want to do is integrate the mainstream into Special Education! (Not such a bad idea. Every child, after all, is 'special'.)

The children react so positively because I've succeeded in getting them to look at literacy from a different point of view. They can struggle with reading and writing, and still walk tall. They know they may have other talents, and they know their classmates know it too.

The other talents are real, but for years I didn't guess at their existence. As always, it was a parent who set me on the right track. Once parents had realized I knew how much I didn't know about dyslexia, but that I was passionately interested in exploring all possible ways of helping their children, they began treating me like a human being, instead of like an 'authority'. Ashley's mother rang up one evening. (Ashley was another student whose writing was indecipherable, but he could design computer programmes as if he were composing a symphony.) "Felicity," she said excitedly, "did you watch *Horizon*?" Curses, curses, no I hadn't. What was it about? "Well, it was about dyslexia, and it was so positive – it was about all the things dyslexics are good at, for a change! Did you know that many great architects are dyslexic? And sculptors? And chess players? And computer programmers?! Ashley sat watching it like a cat that has swallowed the cream. It did him the world of good."

This was fascinating. All my students were brilliant, of course, I was convinced of that, but why architecture, particularly? Why sculpture, and chess? What was the common theme, the connecting link – or was it just coincidence? I was already familiar with Orton's work, and the idea that literacy problems resulted from a confusion of the images perceived in both hemispheres of the brain. Could it be that something which was such a liability in one respect was an asset in others? Time to sit down and ponder.

I pondered. It was when two images merged and overlapped that written words went haywire. But it's when two images merge that we see 'in the round', stereoscopically. I harked back to the intriguing picture books of my childhood, printed in red and green. You looked at them through coloured plastic lenses, and the images leapt from the page. Without the lenses, they were flat and double edged again. Was it possible that dyslexics were visualizing *in three dimensions*? And not just written words, but space and form? That would explain the gift for architecture, sculpture, drawing and painting, electronics, chess. Einstein and Churchill, I knew, were said to have been dyslexic. And Einstein visualized reality not just in two dimensions, not just in three, but in four at least, and possibly in many more. Churchill could review every theatre of the second world war in a single mental glance . . .

A new world opened in front of me. I began to look at what my students were doing, all over again. Here was a child with mirror image spelling and chaotic handwriting. The received wisdom was that he lacked the necessary co-ordination and motor skills to form his letters properly. *So how could the same child move his pencil so fluently over the page when it came to drawing?* And here was another, and another. Edward floundered desperately when he tried to write, but felt tip painting was a different matter. Blocks of shape and colour that balanced in perfect harmony, instinctively arranged with an artist's eye, and pen.

Edward.

How could I have been so blind? My walls are covered, now, with drawings and paintings and designs by all my students, Edward, Lee, Ben, Martin, Barry, Toby, Robert, Darrell, John, Christian, Chris, Nikki, Claire, Guy, Ian, Jason, Jonathan, Sarah. . .

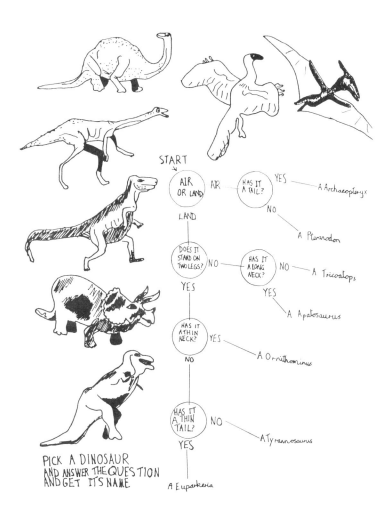

START

AIR OR LAND — AIR — HAS IT A TAIL? — YES — A Archaeopteryx

NO — A Pteranodon

LAND

DOES IT STAND ON TWO LEGS? — NO — HAS IT A LONG NECK? — NO — A Tricolops

YES — A Apatosaurus

YES

HAS IT A THIN NECK? — YES — A Ornithominus

NO

HAS IT A THIN TAIL? — NO — A Tyrannosaurus

YES

PICK A DINOSAUR AND ANSWER THE QUESTION AND GET ITS NAME

A Euparkeria

Lee's spelling is the bane of his life. Fortunately he too watched the *Horizon* programme that I missed: with a lengthening smile, and then he

79

went to fetch his mother. "You must watch this, Mum," he instructed gently, sitting her down in front of the screen. "It's about me." Lee does the 'impossible' drawings – the blocks of wood that go in opposite directions depending on which way you look at them. Or he spends hours drawing patterns of cubes that recede one minute, stand out the next, as your perception shifts. His favourite subject, however, is dinosaurs. What he doesn't know about dinosaurs is not worth knowing, and he can classify them minutely, down to the last wrinkle of skin or menacing claw. Lee and I did a *Headwork* exercise together which involved identifying insects by means of a flow chart. He didn't enthuse particularly, he felt it should have been about dinosaurs. Since he could find nothing along those lines in any of the four books, the following week he brought in the exercise he would like to have done. (See page 79.)

I studied his work, absorbed. The theme was now becoming familiar: not only the skill in drawing, but the feeling for shape and pattern and logical progression. "Lee, this is beautiful, can I put it in my book? And the cube one, and the blocks one?" "Oh yes Miss, if you want." He places his compositions, with loving care, on a high shelf, for me to find when I need them.

'They cannot concentrate, these children,' is more received wisdom; and it is true that some days, when you are working with them, what you say doesn't seem to register because they are elsewhere, marching to a different drum. (Other days they come storming back, and bowl you over with the insights they have garnered on their travels.) But concentration? I go round to have a chat with Ben's Mum, because she lives nearby and this makes more sense than a formal session at the school. While we talk, eleven year old Ben is stretched full length on the floor, working on his picture of a goose. For an hour and a half he concentrates, oblivious to everything around him, now and then going to fetch a tin of white enamel, or gold for the eggs. He cleans his brush carefully between the colours. At last he sits back on his heels and looks at what he has done. He returns to the world of people. "Do you like it, Miss?" "Yes I do, Ben, very much. I don't suppose you would bring it in to school and let me put it on the wall?" "If you want Miss, I'll bring it in tomorrow, when it's dry." So now, when I am tempted to bewail any child's lack of concentration, I have Ben's goose to remind me.

81

82

I begin to tell other parents about what is happening, so they too can discover the bright side of their special children. Avadne, like me, finds it an eye opener. Last year she and I worked with Darren, a fourth year, who had grown increasingly demoralized because of his spelling. (He perked up when I told him he was in illustrious company, and kept mentioning Einstein and Churchill at strategic intervals). He swooshed through a diagnostic dictation, working out most of the memory boosters himself, and began to think he was someone who could, rather than someone who couldn't. Other teachers remarked that he was now writing with confidence, and at length, and his spelling had improved dramatically. What was happening? Ask his Mum, I said smugly, ask Avadne, she's the one who's done it. Now Avadne thinks back to Darren's earlier years. "He loved Lego, and meccano, and things like that. And I tell you what, Felicity, we could never understand it – he used to do jigsaw puzzles for fun, with the *reverse side uppermost!* I didn't think of connecting that with his wonky spelling, though."

Of course she didn't, not just with the one child. No more did I, with any number of students. Nor do the experts and authorities and Special Needs Advisers. Now, thanks to a *Horizon* programme I didn't see, and parents who wanted to help, I know that these talents and skills are most assuredly 'part of the territory', and all we have to do is look out for them, and *point them out to the child.* Often he doesn't know they are there either, he is so used to thinking of himself as someone of no account, just a struggler. He needs to know, he needs to be told.

My daughter Gwynneth, grown up now and an artist herself, a telephone call away, is intrigued by what she calls 'Mum's passion'. I natter at length to her on the phone, and she can see what I can't. I tell her about Jonathan's snake. The head glares fiercely, hanging from the top of the page, fangs poised to strike. At the bottom of the page the tip of the snake's tail appears. "Isn't that lovely," I say, "the rest of the snake isn't there at all, it exists only in his imagination." "Oh mother," declares Gwynneth patiently, "don't you know where the rest of the snake is? It's on the other side of the page, of course!" Of course.

Another time the phone jangles again. "Mother, you must watch the Q.E.D. programme in fifteen minutes, it's right up your street." I watch obediently (I was going to anyway). 'The Foolish Wise Ones' – les idiots savants. Three people forcing their way through one tiny chink in the barriers hedged around them, all with unbelievable gifts. The third brings me to the edge of my seat. He's a severely limited autistic child, but he can draw any of London's buildings from memory, in perfect perspective.[11] A fellow practitioner says that he's probably the most brilliant child artist living in Britain. "Look at that – most artists have to convey perspective by means of shading. Stephen does it all with lines, it's amazing." I feel my spine tingle, thinking dyslexia. Will there be any indication? Nobody has mentioned literacy. He is taken to St Pancras' Station, which he has never seen before, and allowed to study it for fifteen minutes. Later, his drawing emerges, shape, form, detail, depth, solidity, flowing across the page. The only thing wrong with it, say the presenters, baffled, is that he has drawn it the wrong way round.

I leapt back to the phone. "Gwynneth, did you see, he drew St Pancras' Station the wrong way round!" "I know, I know Mum, isn't it exciting!"

Of course he drew St Pancras' Station the wrong way round. And I would lay any money he cannot spell to save his soul.

Footnotes

11. See Stephen Wiltshire, *Drawings*, (Dent).

X

Keeping records

The academic system is wrong about literacy, and it is wrong from the heart. It assumes without question that we should be measuring literacy as performance. Can the child recognize words, can he say them aloud, can he understand them, can he find out the meanings of new words, can he form his letters, can he spell, can he write in sentences, can he use capital letters and full stops and question marks and speech marks, *can he do all this unaided*, can he, can he, can he? We dig around in our children's minds at seven, and eleven, and fourteen, and sixteen, and god knows how many ages in between, desperately measuring their achievements as if they were so many performing seals. We deal in grubby and barren notions, the parameters of our efforts are the lines of success and failure, our watchwords are 'norms', 'monitoring', 'assessment' and 'accountability'.

But all we have to do is to step through the looking glass, take our courage in both hands, and start walking in the opposite direction. Performance doesn't matter, and it never has. What we should be trying to measure is the child's experience. Has he experienced a book that invades his heart and sets his mind on fire? If not, let us try to give him that experience. Has he had the experience of reading aloud successfully? If not, let us try to convince him he can do it. Has he had the experience of seeing the ideas in his own head set out in written words in front of him, and has he seen that they are good? If not, why should he ever have reason to struggle with the mechanics of writing?

Occasionally teachers from other schools visit to find out what I am doing, and we get on like a house on fire, swapping stories about the children we work with, until the moment that I have been dreading. The conversation becomes serious. "What about Assessment, though, Felicity? What about Accountability?" (You can hear the capital A's in their voices.) "Do you keep files for the statemented children?"

My heart sinks. You are supposed to keep a file for every statemented[12] child, pinpointing what he has achieved and what he hasn't, because only in this manner can you find out whether or not your teaching is effective, and what you should do with him next. But I shake my head. "No I don't, not in the way you mean. They are far too time consuming, and I have more important things to do." Their faces are a picture: shock, horror – and then delight. No files. What a lovely idea. Think of what you could do with all that time. "You must keep some records, though?"

"Oh yes. I used to test their reading quite religiously, until I realized the scores told me nothing. They tell you the children who can, but not the children who do. Now I keep lists of the books every child has experienced, with the child's own assessment of whether he has enjoyed the books or not. It sounds haphazard, and unscientific, but it isn't. I just have to look at each child's name, and if there's a great long list of books, most of them with five stars, I know I don't have to worry about him, he's well on the way to becoming a real reader. If there are only a few books, with two or three stars for each one, somebody has got to start reading to that child with all possible speed."

They digest this idea slowly, feeling their way around it. "Mmm – what about writing skills?"

"I do have a diagnostic dictation for each child, because we work our way through those, to give the students the experience of getting a piece of writing perfectly correct.[13] Mainly, I keep copies of all their stories and poems, whether something has been dictated to me, or they've written it out themselves. If they do a good story, we go through it and think of memory boosters for the wonky spellings, which they learn – and I keep a record of those. This means we often have two drafts for a piece of writing, and that's really interesting. It's also good preparation for doing coursework, later."

After the visitors have gone, I find I can articulate my philosophy in a single sentence. For years I have been struggling to find a way of teaching in the classroom like a parent, not like a teacher. Now that I've found it, I'm keeping the sort of records that a parent would keep, not a teacher. I still have records of the books I shared with my daughters when they were little, and the stories and poems they wrote. These are the chronicles that matter, and endure; they chart the experience of a journey.

Here are some mileposts along the way, for the children I am working with now. They are pieces of written work, all of it out of their heads, dictated to me or on to a tape recorder; then usually typed or copied out again by the authors.

'Computer' is Edward's poem, written five months after he began secondary school (see other examples of his work). Before Edward could decide for himself that he wanted to crack the spelling problem, he had to be aware of his own potential, and that the ideas in his head were worth the writing down. This sort of experience, it seems to me, must precede, rather than follow, any formal work on spelling. For this piece of writing, Edward had to pretend to *be* something interesting. He could be a living creature: a particular kind of tree or plant; or an animal – a fox, a hedgehog, an owl, a racehorse. Or he could decide to be a mechanical object: a computer, a telephone, a tractor, a robot, or a ten ton truck. Once he had thought himself into his new persona, I asked him various questions about himself, writing down his replies in cursive handwriting. Edward copied this out in pencil, and afterwards went over it in pen.

13.2.86.

computer

my head is square
inside my head
things are clicking
Bumping
Scratching.
On my face
Numbers
Letters
words
popping up.
In front of me
Buttons pressing down
And clicking up
The letters

Edward Dart

Four months later came 'The Boxbit'. It was Edward's English essay exam at the end of his first year; his teacher enlisted my help. The topic given was 'The Trap', and Edward described to me the odd looking creature caught in the pit he had dug. (He seems to have a liking for strange beasts!) I didn't write down his account. We agreed on each sentence between us, orally, and I dictated it back to him, helping with spelling and punctuation, and making sure he formed the letters correctly. Some spellings – e.g. 'camouflage' – I just provided; and I talked him through others. E.g. 'badger': "Make it say 'bu', what letter do you think? No, good try, but not an 'e', you want an 'a'. Now make it say 'bad' – 'd', well done – and 'd' begins with a rainbow. Now you want two letters to make it say 'badge' – no, you would *think* it was a 'j', wouldn't you, but the word is going to be awkward and have a 'g' instead, and *then* an 'e' so it will make a 'ju' sound! Now the whole word 'badger' – 'r' – excellent – and you have written it fantastically beautifully! I'm getting so excited about your work, Edward!"

26.6.86   THE BOXBIT   Edward Dart

One day me and my mates were walking in the woods and we were bored, so we dug a pit. We put leaves over it to camouflage it. The next day we found an animal with the legs of a badger, the body of a fox, and the ears of a rabbit. So we called it a boxbit.

Diagnostic dictation

Sarah, 14 years   17.1 86

Late one night my
frend awoke me, saying,
"Would you ingoy a trivell
run in my now helecopter?
          I had skerste
Skramd into my trach sout
Befor we were away.
The Light of the City
glodd Benth; the Stars
adume.   I was Buging
it to wand adout
~~ther ouer~~ Bestanation
when I cort Siat
of ~~a~~ the Sping knief
~~eg~~ eagle and the
Surfis ~~of~~ of wbot
~~my~~ must have been a
tipe of ~~fting s~~ Pling
Sorser wserling rond
use.   We doges shell fly
to avod an acsdont.

90

Falcon

Sarah, 14 years
4.6.1986

My beak is sharp
And curved
My wings are long
Like boomerangs
I fly
And hover,
searching for mice,
baby birds,
Rats,
with my powerful eyesight
When I see my prey
My wings go back
the wings of a jet
And I go darting down
My talons fully stretched
tiny noises from the ground
My wings slow me down
I grab the rat
And rip the flesh from
the bones.

Barry

LARK

Apr '85

Guide Dog - I was investigating D......

One day, as I was walking down
I realised I had the Smell of
Christmas. I then and saw
behind me the charge. Dark's hir
of trained house. I watched my
Dock for an puple from my
Diner to give im I now saw
you chrook be its said saw I
Remembered the Belt of my fan cate
and find it drunch his mate and
feed him back I open the get
with with satisfen he grabDf
in to his own Filed I Send
Sutter thr happy then he was
satth and away from the massy and
neutros

HEDGHOG

March 1986

I'M all phuckly
with bits of brown fur
Next to me.
My spins are like needles
they stop other animals
trying to get to me.
when I feel scared
I roll up into a ball
So all anyone can see
Are my spins
Sticking out
Fat of one end
And thin at the other
I Like drinking milk
with bits of meat
And sometimes insects
I like to live
In a bottom.
In a garden where Barry's Nan
Because I am too slow to cross the Road

Barry, 12 years

Edward's older sister, Sarah, has similar literacy problems, as you can see from her diagnostic dictation, at the age of fourteen. 'Falcon' was dictated to me, and I transcribed it onto handwriting paper. Sarah copied it in pencil, I checked it, and suggested one or two handwriting corrections. She illustrated the finished version with loving care, and we both took pride in the result.

Barry's 'Hedgehog' was written in similar fashion. We talked at length, and informally, about hedgehogs – all the questions coming from me, all the closely observed details and knowledge about a hedgehog's habits from Barry himself. I especially like the bit about a hedgehog's spines being 'fat at one end, and thin at the other' – a very simple detail, but neatly and clearly put. Barry was intrigued when I told him why this is – so that if the hedgehog falls for any distance, the spines are not driven back into its body, but can spread the impact.

```
OWL * * * * * * * * * * * * by ANDREW M HARD

My eyes
Glow in the dark
And are fixed in their sockets.
My head
Can turn right around backwards.
My beak is sharp and pointed
Like the end of a curved knife.
My ears stick up in the air.
I coo in the night
My wings are like arms.
My feathers soft and comfortable.
I eat mice
Rats
Voles
And smaller birds.
When they see me
Hovering over the top of them
They try to run away.
I live in an old barn
I sleep in the day
And wake up in the night
So I can go hunting.

6th March 1986
```

'Owl' and 'Charlie' were typed by their authors, from dictation. At first Martin was embarrassed about his reading and writing difficulties, and reluctant to attend Special Education sessions. 'Charlie' was a watershed. Martin's dad is a taxi driver and introduced the diesel 'London' taxi to Dartmouth, so Martin was bound to imagine himself as a taxi. Rosemary, friend and volunteer, helped him to type out his creation, making all the right noises as his fingers struck the keys, standing back in admiration when it was pinned up on the wall. "It's brilliant Martin – you can *see* it's brilliant." Martin could see; now he's the one who tries to smuggle in mainstream friends. Why shouldn't they grow tall, as well?

Martin, 11 years

Sept. 85

One day, as I wis wallking down rig set. I hud the sawd of trting. I tund a siw be hind me the shaer of a fritten h us. I suche in my pokets for a apple from my binur to geve him I. now wax yoe shad be, I siad so I rmevd the belt of my rien coot and tiea it arad his nake. I lede him back I opend the geet with satusseun in to his feld I was suntull vene happy that naw he was sef away from the rae and dagers trafik

94

CHARLIE.............by MARTIN LYE

I am a taxi.
My name is Charlie.
I'm deep black,
Big and strong,
My engine roars
Like a dragon,
Fan belt speeding away,
Throttle cable stretching.
My wheels are big and black and hefty,
My steering wheel is thin and bumpy,
My windscreen is small and flat.
My windscreen wipers are like oars on a boat,
When one stops the other one carries on.
I tear down the road
Speeding past other cars.
I drink diesel,
I sleep on a big hill
Outside my driver's house.

5. 3 . 86

During his second year, I spent time doing *Headwork* [14] exercises with Martin, which gave him the confidence to tackle them on his own. Here is some of his unaided work (see following page):

95

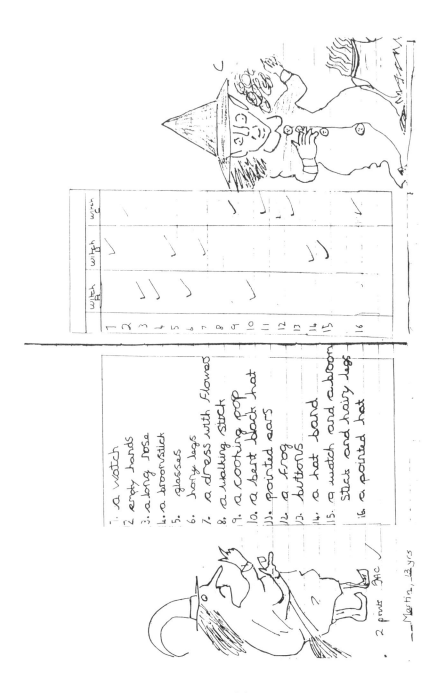

	witch A	witch B	witch C
1	✓		
2	✓		
3	✓✓		✓
4			
5	✓		
6			
7		✓	✓
8			✓
9	✓		✓
10			
11			
12			
13			
14			
15		✓✓	✓
16			

1. a watch
2. empty hands
3. a long nose
4. a broomstick
5. glasses
6. hairy legs
7. a dress with flowers
8. a walking stick
9. a cooking pop
10. a bent black hat
11. pointed ears
12. a frog
13. buttons
14. a hat band
15. a watch and a broom stick and hairy legs
16. a pointed hat

2 from Jac ✓

Martin, 13 yrs

We were the wrong school for Lee (a different Lee). He couldn't understand why school had to impinge on his freedom at all, and with enormous dogged obstinacy, most days he refused to act as if it were really there. This led to considerable conflict in his mainstream lessons, for the teachers and other children had long ago given in and accepted that school was real. In class he was a little devil, but with Rosemary he was an angel, washing his hands obediently before approaching the typewriter, sitting up straight, refusing to look at the keyboard, making his fingers find the right letters by touch alone. ("How do you do it, Rosemary?" I asked enviously. He tolerated me, just, but I had nothing like the same rapport. She thought about it. "I'm not a teacher, I'm fierce with them and won't stand any nonsense, but they know I love them and think they're brilliant." That just about summed it up.) Lee had typically chaotic handwriting and spelling, and was one of the ones who set me thinking when he spent hours illustrating his 'Laddie' poem. He longed for a dog, and Laddie was the dog he wished he could have had.

MY DOG . . . . by LEE BERRY

My name is Laddie
My fur is blondish brown.
I like swimming in the sea
When it is rough.
It feels like a bath
But it is much rougher.
I like running in the woods
On the soft grass
And the hard mud.
I like chewing bones
And burying them.
My master is Lee
I like chasing after him,
And at night I sleep at the end of his bed.

20th February 1986.

27.6.85

flights ✓ / incorrectings
sundaes ✓ / delight
suppestion d / in directory
ugaligy / in wordwork
wright / in wordwork
misinformation
argument ✓
probably ✓
amiss ✓
10...

Darrell, 12 yrs

Darrell 11 yrs

7th Sept 1984

Diagnostic — Picturing

a day,

os I was working off - dawn
previsley, I had the sound os
chating + tunk and I was plaindme-
frm shoge Dark here os A friting
litl hous
I subngol in my pokits for An
appwl. From my diner + o gave hem
4 I no wer shiud D ... I sotd.
So I fouw the pelt ... os my fince
and tip it grod hes neti and
Lead Hem Park ... 4pind the get
and with satchn he galem t
into hes vella
I was sunthee sirr yappey thts now
in wos soSosu away from nibe
and progth frastrk.

98

Darrell is one of the quiet ones, but he too is more often than not somewhere else. There is a great deal going on in his head, however, as you can see from the colourful imagery and confident use of language in 'Robotic Zizz'. He dictated the piece to me, and I later wrote it out on handwriting paper for him to copy.

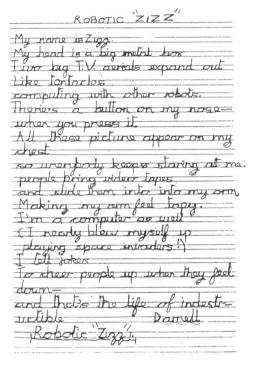

ROBOTIC "ZIZZ"

My name is Zizz.
My head is a big metal box
Two big T.V. aerials expand out
Like tentacles
computing with other robots.
There's a button on my nose—
when you press it.
All those pictures appear on my
chest
so everybody keeps staring at me.
people bring video tapes
and slide them into into my arm.
Making my arm feel tapy.
I'm a computer as well
(I nearly blew myself up
playing space invaders.)
I tell jokes
To cheer people up when they feel
down—
and that's the life of indestr=
uctible   Darrell
Robotic "Zizz".

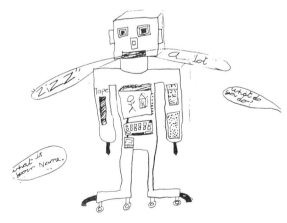

Finally, 'Crimefighter', which I'm including because it illustrates yet another way of enabling a child to break through the barriers. Jason (Darrell's younger brother), started off telling me his story, and then proceeded to dictate it bit by bit. But something was wrong. The mere fact of my presence, and also that I couldn't write fast enough, impeded the flow. Later that day, he asked if he could use the tape recorder. I was thrilled when he played back the result, he'd captured the laconic, insourciant style beautifully, even better than when he'd told me the story in the first instance. I transcribed the piece at leisure, and afterwards typed it out for him. (The only bit I was doubtful about was that his Dad didn't actually say "What the hell are you doing here?" "I'm sorry, Jason, I don't think we can get away with using *that* word. You will have to tone it down." Jason grinned ruefully, but obliged.)

CRIMEFIGHTER . . . . . by JASON, 12 years

One day, walking down the road, by myself, you know how it is – just me, myself, on my own – school in a couple of minutes. In school, boredom as usual, three o'clock, went home, watched TV. Well, hope you're taking this in, this leads to a really great story.

Went out for a walk, this car zoomed past me, smacked into a hedge, and blew up. All this money was flying everywhere – I mean, what would you do with all this money floating around in the air? You would probably pick it up, that's what I done. Then I found a suitcase and it had loads of money in it, man really heavy stuff, lots of five pound notes. I was scared stiff, I didn't know what to do, so I picked it up and ran for it.

The police car came, so I hid behind a hedge. Police saw the money and the car being burnt up and one said it was a bank robbery.

I wondered what to do – come out from behind the bush, give them the money, or what? Because if I tried to give them the money and explain, they would think I was in with the bunch.

What should I do now? I had to clear my name. Should I go down to the bank and give it back, say I found it? So I started walking down town. I got picked up by the police, this was no laughing matter.

They took me down to the station, and phoned up my parents. I was scared stiff, I wondered what they were going to do. I kept saying I just found the money, but they didn't believe me.

Dad came down and said, "What the hell are you doing here?" I said, "Nothing, Dad." Then the bank manager rang up and said it wasn't me, so the police said I could go home with my Dad.

Next day, school, boredom as usual, people asking me why I was down at the police station last night.

A week later, another car zoomed past me and tipped over. More money floating out of it. This time I wasn't going to be a hero. I jumped on the bus and went home. I learned my lesson, not to be a crime fighter. It could get you in a lot of trouble.

Jason

Footnotes

12. A 'statemented' child is one who has been issued with a statement of special educational needs by the local authority, specifying the provision that must be made for him.

13. These are taken from Margaret Peters' *A Diagnostic and Remedial Spelling Manual* (Macmillan Education)

14. See p.101

A book list for you

Susanne Langer, *Philosophy in a New Key: A Study in the Study in the Symbolism of Reason, Rite and Art* (Harvard University Press, 1942)

'Modern theories of meaning usually culminate in a critique of science. Susanne Langer's work presents a study of human intelligence beginning with a semantic theory, and leading into a critique of art . . .'

Mrs Langer is therefore the artist's philosopher, and her sources are the descriptions which artists themselves have used to try to portray in words what it is they are about. She rings true in a way many philosophers do not.

Setting the stage for her later analysis of the various art forms, she goes straight to the heart of the artistic vision in her discussion of metaphor. Since this makes clear just why recording a child's natural metaphors is such a powerful way of unlocking his perceptions, it is worth quoting at length:

> 'Where a precise word is lacking to designate the novelty which the speaker would point out, he resorts to the powers of *logical analogy*, and uses a word denoting something else that is a presentational symbol for the thing he means; the context makes it clear that he cannot mean the thing literally denoted, and must mean something else symbolically. For instance, he might say of a fire: "It flares up," and be clearly understood to refer to the action of the fire. But if he says: "The king's anger flares up," we know from the context that "flaring up" cannot refer to the sudden appearance of a physical flame; it must connote the idea of "flaring up" as a *symbol* for what the king's anger is doing. We conceive the literal meaning of the term that is usually used in connection with a fire, but this concept serves us here as proxy for another which is nameless. The expression "to flare up" has acquired a wider meaning than its original use, to describe the behaviour of a flame; it can be used metaphorically to describe

whatever its *meaning* can symbolize.

'In a genuine metaphor an image of the literal meaning is our symbol for the figurative meaning, the thing that has no name of its own. If we say that a brook is laughing in the sunlight, an idea of laughter intervenes to symbolize the spontaneous, vivid activity of the brook. But if a metaphor is used very often, we learn to accept the word in its metaphorical context as though it had a literal meaning there. If we say: "The brook runs swiftly," the word "runs" does not connote any leg-action, but a shallow rippling flow. If we say that a rumor runs through the town, we think neither of leg-action nor of ripples; or if a fence is said to run round the barnyard there is not even a connotation of changing place. Originally these were probably all metaphors but one (though it is hard to say which was the primitive literal sense). Now we take the word itself to mean *that which all its applications have in common,* namely *describing a course.* The great extent and frequency of its metaphorical services have made us aware of the basic concept by virtue of which it can function as a symbol in so many contexts; constant figurative use has generalized its sense.

'Wegener calls such a word a "faded metaphor," and shows that all general words are probably derived from specific appellations, by metaphorical use; so that our literal language is a very repository of "faded metaphors" . . .

'Metaphor is our most striking evidence of *abstractive seeing,* of the power of human minds to use presentational symbols. Every new experience, or new idea about things, evokes first of all some metaphorical expression. As the idea becomes familiar, this expression "fades" to a new literal use of the once metaphorical predicate, a more general use then it had before. It is in this elementary, presentational mode that our first adventures in conscious abstraction occur. The spontaneous similes of language are our first record of *similarities* perceived. The fact that poverty of language, need of emphasis, or need of circumlocution for any reason whatever, leads us at once to seize upon a metaphorical word, shows how natural the perception of

103

common form is, and how easily one and the same concept is conveyed through words that represent a wide variety of conceptions. The use of metaphor can hardly be called a conscious device. It is the power whereby language, even with a small vocabulary, manages to embrace a multimillion things; whereby new words are born and merely analogical meanings become stereotyped into literal definitions. (Slang is almost entirely far-fetched metaphor. Although much of it is conscious and humorous in intent, there is always a certain amount of peculiarly apt and expressive slang which is ultimately taken into the literary language as "good usage".)

'One might say that, if ritual is the cradle of language, metaphor is the law of its life. It is the force that makes it essentially *relational*, intellectual, forever showing up new, abstractable *forms* in reality, forever laying down a deposit of old, abstracted concepts in an increasing treasure of general words.

'The intellectual vocabulary grows with the progress of conceptual thinking and civilized living. Technical advances make demands on our language which are met by the elaboration of mathematical, logical and scientific terminologies . . . Speech becomes increasingly discursive, practical, prosaic, until human beings can actually believe that it was invented as a utility, and was later embellished with metaphors for the sake of a cultural product called poetry . . .' (Pp. 139-142)

Huges Mearns, *Creative Power: The Education of Youth in the Creative Arts* (Dover Publications, 1958; 1st ed. 1929)

All the best books are out of print! The headmaster of the school where I first taught lent me *Creative Power,* and I promptly bought my own copy. It has pointed the way ever since. Hughes Mearns believes utterly in the creative potential of all children, and spent his life as a teacher evoking its expression. *Creative Power* is a testament to the children he knew and worked with: its pages are studded with their work. But one passage especially stays with me when I am tempted to lose heart. An Important

Personage descended on his classroom, demanding to see results. He tried to shush her, she was interrupting the children, but she refused to be shushed:

> '"I have a good stopwatch in my desk," I whispered, and pointed through the window to Morningside Park. "Do take it and go out, right away into Morningside Park. Sit down on the grass for an hour and time the dandelions. As the seconds tick away, watch their growth and then come back and report to me. Do you know what you will say? Exactly nothing has happened."
>
> 'I found the watch in my desk and tried in dramatic whispers to press it upon her. She edged away from me. I stalked her. "Do go out and time the dandelions!" I begged. But she would not. She did not speak. She would not even stay. She went quickly away from there.' (P. 35)

He offers another of the paradoxes that refresh the traveller. We have been told so forcefully and for so long that if we wish to be good teachers we must love teaching, we must steep ourselves in child development, we must be masters of methodology. Mearns indicates that although teaching interests him he wouldn't willingly give up a meal for it. What he loves, and passionately, is the *practice of writing*. 'I am a writing man,' he says, 'and not a teacher of writing; and there is a vast difference between these two sorts of creature . . .'

Liz Waterland makes a similar observation: 'It is a sad fact that many teachers are not truly literate themselves; they can read but are not readers, which is why so many of their children will never be readers either.'(*Read With Me* and After, *Signal* 51, September 1986.)

But if we put books first, and writing first, the children will follow, and flourish, though we have opened never a book on child development in our lives.

Sandy Brownjohn, *Does It Have To Rhyme*? (Hodder and Stoughton, 1980) and *What Rhymes With Secret*? (Hodder and Stoughton, 1982)

Since poetry comes first, and prose comes tumbling after, these books are at the secret heart of literacy. They are meant as handbooks for teachers of the 9-15 age group; but the ideas and feeling for language which they convey will inform work with children of any age. This is what it's all for, here are the keys of the kingdom.

Betty Edwards, *Drawing on the Right Side of the Brain,* (Fontana/Collins, 1982; lst ed. 1979)

Betty Edwards is a working artist and art teacher. She discovered as a child that her skill in drawing was not so much a matter of what she did with her hands. It depended on a different way of looking at objects. She had to 'see' them artistically: not as 'things', but as arrangements of colour, shape and form. All of us, she maintains, can see with an artist's vision, but to do so we must learn to ignore the rational, direct, literal perceptions of the brain's left hemisphere, and start 'drawing on the right side of the brain' where the ways of knowing are intuitive, imaginative, relational and holistic. This seems to me to offer a further insight into the talents of dyslexic children. If they are already 'drawing on the right side of the brain' to a much greater extent than the rest of us, they may have access to the artistic way of seeing more readily and naturally.

Betty Edward's book contains a wealth of fascinating ideas and suggestions which enable anyone to tap into their creative side, and gain pleasure from artistic expression.

Annabel Thomas, *The Usborne First Guide to The BBC Micro,* (Usborne Publishing, 1984)

If you thought you couln't understand computers . . .

Joan Duffy, *Type it,* (Better Books, 1974)

A helpful typing manual, designed specifically for children with literacy problems.

Bevé Hornsby and Frula Shear, *Alpha to Omega,* (Heinemann Educational, 1974)

The two authors have specialized in teaching dyslexics. They point out that 'the roots of the ideas that form the basis of the programme lie in the work of Anne Gillingham and Bessie Stillman, who, in conjunction with Samuel T. Orton, began to devise a phonetically based scheme for the teaching of dyslexics in the 1930s'. Just don't think of *Alpha to Omega* as a 'reading' course – but what it will do is to help a dyslexic tally written words with spoken words *while* he reads. This in turn will help him to tally the words back again, and so crack the spelling problem.

It's interesting that the authors also think their programme works by identifying 'what it is that the dyslexic finds so difficult, and training and shaping these weaknesses so that they are overcome'. In fact they have identified what he finds comparatively *easy* to do! – that is, pronouncing spoken words accurately, and tallying them with shapes. By concentrating on this route to spelling, *Alpha to Omega* observes Frank Smith's dictum, and makes learning to spell easy, rather than difficult. (A slog, admittedly, but at least the path is clear.)

Marlene Morris, *Solve Your Spelling Problems*, (Pitman 1982)

Once a child is adept at phonic translation, and can spell 'regular' words with ease, he can move on to tackling the irregular ones. Marlene Morris's book is excellent for use with teenagers. It works on a system of 'memory boosters' for irregular words, similar to my own. The author has developed her programme as a result of fifteen years experience of teaching business English to adult students, but don't expect a dreary diet of "In reply to yours of the fifth instant'! The vocabulary presented is a rich and literate one, and the sentences given as examples are themselves an education in general knowledge. It's a good idea for the student to practise typing some of the sentences: he will be consolidating his grasp of spelling, and extending his general knowledge, while he types. The book can be used with a helper, or as a self teaching programme.

Chris Culshaw and Deborah Waters, *Headwork*, Books 1, 2, 3 and 4, (Oxford University Press, 1984)

We may all be poets, but prose does have its place; and sooner or later we have to get to grips with textbook work. This is a delightful series which gives even the strugglers the experience of success. It lends itself to a shared exploration by adult and child, and deals in logical puzzles, Cloze

107

procedure, matching, sequencing, flow charts, riddles . . . I let my students pick any exercise that takes their fancy, from any of the books, and to begin with we read and talk about the exercise together. When the child has decided how to tackle it, I will often dictate his answers back to him, using memory boosters for tricky words to give him the feeling of spelling independently, and reminding him about handwriting and punctuation when necessary. (He writes in pencil so he can correct any mistakes.) The result is usually something we can both be proud of; then he illustrates it.

Reference materials

Finding the correct spelling for a word in your head can be a daunting project for a child with spelling problems. How can you set about finding it in a dictionary if you're not sure what it looks like? The *ACE Spelling Dictionary*, by David Moseley and Catherine Nicol (LDA, 1986) triumphantly shows any child a way around the barrier. ACE stands for 'Aurally Coded English', and if you can sound out the word, you can find it in this dictionary. The 16,000 words are grouped according to the first strong vowel sound. Prefix this with what you think is the initial letter, turn to the correct page, count the number of syllables – and there it is. You really can find any word in 30 seconds, as the authors claim. The index enabling you to accomplish this feat covers only two pages, and is beautifully clear and easy to use. (You have permission to photocopy the index, which is handy.)

Even more fun to use, and also vastly more expensive, is the *Franklin Spellmaster*, a mini spelling computer available from McIntyre House, Canning Place, Liverpool, L70 1AX. Franklin has a vocabulary of 70,000 words, nearly twice the number of words used by the most verbose author in the English language (who you might have thought was Shakespeare, but turns out to be Edgar Allen Poe, according to the blurb). Use the QWERTY keyboard to enter any word, and if you have a reasonable phonetic approximation, Franklin will search his memory, and display the correct version. If that isn't the one you want, scroll down through a list of related words, until you find it. You can also play games like 'Hangman' and 'Anagrams', or cheat on crosswords! Little larger than a pocket calculator,

Franklin costs about £60, which isn't really expensive when you reflect that it is in fact a computer. Also, any child who possesses Franklin will be the envy of his peers, who will all be clamouring to borrow it and 'have a go'. Every incentive, therefore, to be relaxed about spelling, and to get in the habit of checking the spellings of all doubtful words.

G. Solomons, *Spell It,* (Macmillan Education, 1980)

This is actually a spelling list, containing 8,000 words; inexpensive at about £1, and a handy pocket size. The layout is clear and legible. The words are listed alphabetically, but as no meanings are given (except where it is necessary to distinguish between homonyms) it really isn't difficult to find the word you want. Virtually all the words a school child would need are included, and related words are conveniently grouped together (e.g. ice, icicle, icily, icy). A *Spell It* could well be used in conjunction with Franklin, or the *ACE Spelling Dictionary.* Once the correct spelling of a word has been discovered, a child could practise finding it in a *Spell It*, thus becoming familiar with works of reference arranged in alphabetical order.

When a word has been found in any work of reference, it should never be copied 'letter by letter'. The student should scrutinize it carefully to decide on the tricky bits, and then work out a way of saying it to himself which will give him the spelling. (This is often simply a matter of *saying* silent letters, including saying doubled letters twice.) E.g. 'p-ne-u-monia' for 'pneumonia', 'web-bed' for ' webbed', 'rē-li-ĕf' for 'relief'. Then the student writes the whole word out of his head, saying the memory booster to himself as he does so.

You will notice that we have simply inserted one additional, vital step into the LOOK, COVER, WRITE, CHECK routine. 'Looking' on its own will not help. But LOOK, <u>SAY</u>, COVER, WRITE, CHECK will do the job. By this means, the student will be developing the 'saying way of looking' at words, until it becomes virtually automatic; and steadily compiling a 'saying-for-spelling' vocabulary in the process. As this vocabulary grows, he should find increasingly that he can spell more and more words 'out of his head', without having to check them, and this does wonders for his self confidence.

The *Longman Concise English Dictionary* (Longman, 1985)

Of course, the real purpose of a dictionary is not to standardize spelling, but to crystallize the meanings of words by focusing on their common usage. The great dictionaries of the English language are works of art in themselves, and many children who fall in love with words will browse through dictionaries just for pleasure, curling their tongue around the strangest entries because they look and sound so delightful. The meanings of words grow organically; roots, prefixes and suffixes leap from word to word, often through audacious metaphorical twists that leave one breathless with discovery. For example, the Latin root 'flare' means 'blow', giving the verb 'inflare' and the past participle 'inflatus'. Its descendants re-emerge in our own 'flare' and 'inflate', but an 'inflated' personage is not a fat person, but someone whose idea of himself is so puffed up that he is just about to pop with self importance!

Any child should be able to appreciate the family history of words, and to have some idea of the countless tributaries and rivers which flow into the mighty ocean of the modern English language. A specific awareness of how the different building blocks of words can be realigned, combined, permuted, is an enriching experience. The child realizes that he too can generate words, just as his forebears have done: he can not only make things with words, but make new things that *are* words, using the heritage of many peoples and many tongues to do so. This, to me, is the real reason why Latin used to be part of the 'core corriculum', and the fascinating thing is that it is by no means dead yet. A third of Britain's state schools still teach Latin and Greek, and some to all students – *including* those with literacy problems! – in a modern, racy, imaginative way. Nobody ploughs through the arid wastes of *De Bello Gallico* any more.

Adrian Spooner, at Park View Comprehensive School in County Durham, is pioneering a fresh approach to the classics. His lessons begin with a story (usually pleasantly blood curdling) to stimulate discussion, go on to word building using Greek and Latin roots, and end up with basic English grammar. As a result, students find themselves understanding the actual meaning of words like 'computer' or 'photosynthesis', and breezily coin new

110

words themselves ('tempiphone' for the 'speaking clock', or 'miktophone' for a multi-linguist). This sort of approach is just what students with literacy problems (especially) need, as it offers them a means of getting to grips with words at their very heart, and so realizing that they can be the ones in command. It was first tried in Indianapolis, and, within five months, the American pupils were ahead of a control group by a year in reading, seven months in maths computation, nine months in maths concept, and five months in science. (If you're interested, the text book *Lingo*, by Adrian Spooner, should by now be available from Bristol Classical Press).

But we digress! I started off talking about dictionaries. A good dictionary should arouse the apprentice's interest in the basic structure and formation of words. So it has to identify roots, prefixes and suffixes, with some indication of where they come from.

The *Longman Concise English Dictionary* has more than 50,000 headwords and 100,000 definitions, plus over 100 full page illustrations. It's up-to-date on every subject, and it gives the genealogy of all words. The print is helpfully spaced and easy to read. At around £10 it is excellent value. It seems to me a good idea to provide your child with something portable when he just needs to find spellings, but to go for something more comprehensive when it's a matter of tracking down the meanings of words. The *Longman Concise* is a work you can keep at home and explore with your child.

An enjoyable method of tackling a dictionary together is to play 'Call My Bluff'. Each of you in turn chooses a real horror of a word, and invents two false meanings for it, which are offered alongside the real one. Your opponent tries to guess the true meaning, and you win if he plumps for a false one. This is a creative way of playing with words and meanings, and should go far towards removing many of the imagined terrors of a dictionary. The book comes to be seen as a pleasant friend and servant, rather than as an incomprehensible jungle of words.